D1506398

ENDORSEMENTS

In this wise book, Dana Look-Arimoto reframes work-life balance for the 21st century. She argues for a more well-rounded way of looking at career, family, friendships, community, and vitality using a deliberate and self-aware method of making the choices that are right for you. This book is a much-needed call for sanity and a real breath of fresh air for anyone who's feeling overwhelmed.

-Daniel H. Pink, author of WHEN and DRIVE

"Want to create an energizing, successful life? Dana's amazing book gives you the 5 facets to rediscover the brilliant you. In a clear, insightful model, she helps you see where you may have unconsciously settled for less in your life and helps you create a Journey Map to unleash your power. Her vast experience combined with her passion for cutting through the derailers gives you the strategy, courage and tools to get off the hamster wheel and reclaim your life. Read and cherish it today!"

**-Dr. Vicki Halsey, VP Applied Learning,
Ken Blanchard Companies**

"Wow! How refreshing it was to hear what I've been thinking for so long, "Is there really such a thing as work-life balance?" With my crazy, hectic life, Dana's frank approach to settling smart, "accept who you are and decide consciously how you want to spend your time, instead of stressing over how you should be spending your time" was just what I needed to hear"

-Chip Conley, *New York Times* bestselling author of *Emotional Equations*, Airbnb Head of Global Hospitality & Strategy

"Redesign Your Busy Life." Great concept! We design our homes, we wear designer clothes and accessories. At work, we design custom solutions for our clients. We are often so busy designing our outer worlds, but how skilled are we at designing our inner worlds. Dana deftly gets you to pause and think about the decisions you make and how you can live your life by design."

-Nadia Bilchik, CNN Editorial Producer.
President Greater Impact Communication

"Work-life balance? There is only one life, and face it, we are all constantly working! How to manage it all? That's the question that Dana answers in this marvelous book! It is a clear guide to a happier healthier and more productive life."

-Chester Elton Global Leadership guru, and NYT Best-selling author of *The Carrot Principle*, *ALL In* and *The Best Team Wins*

"As Dana says in her book, this falls into a business meets self-help genre. While I read a lot of business books, I generally don't see a need for self-help books. I thought I'd read this anyway because I was intrigued by the idea of redefining work-life balance. I read the book in one sitting and was delighted that I did. Yes, it is self-help but very pertinent to the business world, and immensely helpful to me personally."

-Linda Sharkey, Marshall Goldsmith 100 Coach,
Best Selling Author of *Is Your Company Future Proof?*

I say a resounding 'YES!' to everything this book cultivates. Dana challenges the work-life balance paradigm to offer a new way of being present in each moment of our day. Read this book if you want to stop saying, "If I only had more time in the day" and start maximizing the time you do have. I promise if you live this truth you will look back on this book as a catalyst for massive personal and professional growth.

-Ryan McCarty, Co-Founder Culture of Good,
Author of *Build A Culture Of Good*

"In these frenetic times, 'work-life balance' seems increasingly out of reach. Dana Look-Arimoto's smart perspective will help you rethink your priorities and make informed choices about how you really want to live your life."

-Dorie Clark, author of *Entrepreneurial You* and *Stand Out*, and
adjunct professor, Duke University Fuqua School of Business

"This book covers every aspect of life. In Dana's words, Career, Generations, Circle, Society, and Vitality. She dissects each aspect and rebuilds them in a unique way. She provides expert advice along with a fun quiz to find your Current and Desired Life Gem. The quiz alone is reason to read this life-changing book."

-Dr. Mark Goulston, Best Selling Author and prominent
psychiatrist and consultant to major organizations

"I loved this book! The title threw me at first, "do I stop settling or do I settle smart?" The way Dana shared her work and life experiences was perfect for explaining what comes in the book's subtitle, it's all about "redesigning" your extremely busy life. I've started doing it and the sense of relief is really welcomed."

-Rajesh Setty, Author of *"Smart, but Stuck"*
and co-founder of Audvisor.com

"What an amazing book! Dana blew the myth of work-life balance right out of the water, and then did a masterful job of explaining how to rethink and redesign your own work-life balance with Smart Settling. The following really resonated with me, "I love what I do in all aspects of my life, and my kids and my family get that. I do not see any evidence of them feeling less than as I am explicit about it. They know I am all in whenever I do anything. That thing I'm focused on gets all of me. And I wouldn't trade that!"

-Holly G. Green, CEO, The Human Factor, Inc.

Settling Smart is being aware of your choices from family to career, friendships, community, and well-being –just how do you want to settle and invest your time without feeling guilty? The book is a quick, entertaining read with just three phases: a method, mindset, and movement –that is movement forward where you are thriving! For me, I have yet to find the work-life balance so my focus has been on work-life integration that is healthy for me and my family.

-Jacqueline M. Stavros, Author of *Conversations Worth Having* and Professor of Management, Lawrence Technological University

Dana Look-Arimoto's passion for assisting people to find contentment while engaging all aspects of their life is clear. Her book is just the first step in what I trust will become a powerful movement as more of us Settle Smart. As a C-level executive, I see every day how employees become disconnected and disengaged when they struggle with the conflicts between the demands of their family and business. Her strategies provide clear and actionable solutions that will enable you to stay engaged and be supported in all spheres by settling smarter.

-Kate Purmal, Author of *The Moonshot Effect* and Winner of Axiom Business Book Awards Gold Medal in Leadership

STOP SETTLING, SETTLE SMART

RETHINKING WORK-LIFE BALANCE, REDESIGN YOUR BUSY LIFE

Dana Look-Arimoto

Stop Settling, Settle Smart Rethinking Work-life Balance, Redesign Your Busy Life Copyright © 2018 by Dana Look-Arimoto.

All rights reserved. No part of this publication may be reproduced, distributed, or transmitted in any form or by any means, including photocopying, recording, or other electronic or mechanical methods, without the prior written permission of the author, except in the case of brief quotations embodied in critical reviews and certain other noncommercial uses permitted by copyright law.

Jones Media Publishing
10645 N. Tatum Blvd. Ste. 200-166
Phoenix, AZ 85028
www.JonesMediaPublishing.com

Disclaimer:

The author strives to be as accurate and complete as possible in the creation of this book, notwithstanding the fact that the author does not warrant or represent at any time that the contents within are accurate due to the rapidly changing nature of the Internet.

While all attempts have been made to verify information provided in this publication, the Author and Publisher assume no responsibility and are not liable for errors, omissions, or contrary interpretation of the subject matter herein. The Author and Publisher hereby disclaim any liability, loss or damage incurred as a result of the application and utilization, whether directly or indirectly, of any information, suggestion, advice, or procedure in this book. Any perceived slights of specific persons, peoples, or organizations are unintentional.

In practical advice books, like anything else in life, there are no guarantees of income made. Readers are cautioned to rely on their own judgment about their individual circumstances to act accordingly. Readers are responsible for their own actions, choices, and results. This book is not intended for use as a source of legal, business, accounting or financial advice. All readers are advised to seek services of competent professionals in legal, business, accounting, and finance field.

Printed in the United States of America

ISBN-13: 978-1-945849-72-5 Paperback
JMP2019.3

DEDICATION

Dedicated to my beloved family, Darren, Ava, and Annika,
and all the fur-babies past, present, and future.

CONTENTS

FOREWORD

Stop Settling, Settle Smart, by Dana Look-Arimoto a
Foreword by John Baldoni

SOME OF US say "yes" to everything. Every request and every opportunity. We're go-getters and achievers who love the thrill of big challenges. And that's great, until it isn't.

Working hard is a laudable American tradition, but so, too, is working long hours. According to the World Tourism Organization, Americans on average take the fewest vacation days of any nation in its report — just 13 paid days a year. Compare that to 42 days for Italian, 37 for French, 35 for German, and 25 for both Korean and Japanese workers.

It's one thing to find success in your career, and another thing to be a fulfilled, healthy, and – yes, successful – person.

The ideal of work-life "balance" instills in us a sense that we must become a superhero in order to feel successful. We have to work (at least one) full-time job, excel in our relationships with family and friends, volunteer in our community, and still have time to exercise, eat right, and pursue hobbies. We believe that giving anything less than our all in every situation means we're a failure in some way.

I know too many people who see compromise as a bad thing, an abandonment of principle. In reality, a willingness to compromise is a sign of great conviction: the conviction of finding one's balance, knowing our strengths and shortcomings, and finding the disposition and courage to wisely spend our time in multiple arenas.

Why do we spend so much of our time on things that won't make us happy? The famous hierarchy of needs, created by psychologist Abraham Maslow, suggests that after covering basic human needs (food, health, friends, and coffee that doesn't come out of a single-button machine), a person will ultimately seek self-actualization. But if you're dumping all your extra energy into one or more of your needs, what energy do you have left to seek happiness? You're saying "yes" way more than "no!"

As you will learn in this book, there is no such thing as work-life "balance," and certainly no variant of that concept which applies to all of us equally. Work isn't an isolated world; we don't change who we are, or how much energy we have, when we sit down at our desks.

Many of us live our lives believing that we must overachieve – not just at the things that matter the most to us, but at everything we do. We must learn that failure comes only when we give in to defeat. There's no failure in placing deliberate limits on the time and energy we put toward each goal, thereby allowing us more energy to spend where we find happiness. You settle, so that you have more. That's not only reasonable, that's smart.

So, why do we think settling is always negative?

As Dana Look-Arimoto writes, it's not just okay but mandatory to ask oneself what you need and want to achieve happiness. What are your goals towards finding the best quality of life? What do you want to spend your energy on? People who fully embrace Stop Settling, Settle Smart learn how to prioritize their time based on what they truly want out of life. They learn how to answer those questions honestly and completely, and they have the courage to start making conscious choices about where to compromise and where to go all-in. They learn where to settle and where to push for more.

We're fooling ourselves if we think we can separate the different facets of our lives as easily as if we were changing clothes. Every aspect of our lives intertwines, and we have a finite amount of energy and time to spend. By making deliberate, conscious choices about the things that matter most to you, the things that matter a little less, and the things you're willing to compromise on, you become the person you want to be. We shouldn't be picking and choosing the things we say "no" to. We should be choosy about the times we say "Yes!"

We all want to feel happy and fulfilled, but how many of us have actually taken the time to define exactly what that means – for all aspects of our lives? And if you have thought about it, did you take the time to figure out how much of your energy is going toward each goal, and why? It's all about active introspection and deliberate compromises. Stop settling involuntarily. Choose your course, and follow your star with purpose. That's how you'll achieve your goal.

The ideal life looks different for everyone, and we all have a unique definition of fulfilment and "success." By consciously choosing your priorities in Career, Generations, Circle, Society, and Vitality, you take the first step toward that goal. No apologies. No guilt.

Accomplished leaders know how to prioritize goals, choosing the critical ones to spend energy on, and delegating – thereby compromising on – the rest. By learning this skill, you'll find that you are actually progressing more quickly and efficiently toward the goals that matter the most. You'll know how and why you choose to do things, and you'll have a structure to determine whether an opportunity is worth your time and passion.

We all know plenty of people who work long hours, internalize tension, and feel that they are responsible for accepting every single opportunity or responsibility offered. You can't be a superhero if you turn things down, right? Well, as Dana knows, that's a myth. You can Settle Smart!

Life is about setting goals that push us to become better than we are. It's an ongoing process of reaching for the stars. Find the things that mean the most to you, and give them the time and energy they deserve. It's not "balance." It's harmony.

The power of settling will change your life.

John Baldoni is an internationally recognized executive coach and educator, and the author of 14 leadership books published in 10 languages world-wide. In 2018 Trust Across America granted John the Lifetime Achievement Award for Trust.

ACKNOWLEDGEMENTS

I NOW UNDERSTAND why acknowledgments are long and difficult to write. There are so many people I want to thank who have influenced, supported, and inspired this entire Method, Mindset, and Movement, manifested into a book. All to help individuals and companies with fit and match, as well as individuals within their holistic, authentic lives.

For starters, I'd like to thank my husband for endless hours of brainstorming, pushing back, helping me clarify and get out of my own head. I love and adore you. You will always be the free space on my Bingo card. You are the calm to my constant storm. My endless source of stability. You are my Zen Buddha. Your ability to see things clearly and with grace is so comforting all the time. You are what keeps me anchored, sailor. An unconditional partnership that I never thought possible, until now.

For my daughters, Ava and Annika. Ava, thank you for being such an empath, always putting others first, and learning that you count, equally and importantly. Keep building your confidence. There's nothing you won't be capable of as long as you believe (do the work!). Annika, you are truly fearless and gifted. Your voice brings me joy. Your passion toward life, friendship, education, and making a difference is always something I can rely on, even when you are plowing through to get to where you want to go. Your heart is always centered at the intention.

The three of you had so much patience for my writing process which is a whirlwind of highs and lows, emotionally and mentally. Thank you for the inspiration. Your wisdom, your emotion, your life events, the way you've grown, my beautiful daughters, are nothing short of awesome. I love all three of you so so much. More than I can ever express.

For my Chief Canine Officer team, that continues to change and shift over years as rescue puppies get older and leave us and new ones enter. I thank them for working with me every day. Their companionship, happiness when seeing me, unconditional love, and endless voracious appetite continue to motivate me. For everyone else, thank you for tolerating their barking.

I don't know how to thank this person, other than to say I would not have the confidence, courage, and commitment to be where I am today if you weren't by my side, supporting me, pushing back, and truly making all of my written word better, more understood, more flow-y and flourish-y, less pragmatic and corporate, and more authentic to who I really am. You help give voice to my word on paper. Yes, Sonia, I'm talking about you.

For my review team, Amelia, Anita, Mike, Peggy, Todd, and Wendy, and for everyone who contributed to my writing process and journey. Either by chapter or complete manuscript, your insight and takeaways have shaped this book and my Movement with your friendship, incredible eye for detail, and feedback. Thank you for being honest, constructive, and validating. From the bottom of my heart, I thank you.

To Jeremy Jones of Jones media, your boot camp kicked my boot in the best possible way. The community you've built that supports authors along their journey is one that I'm sure I will want to repeat whatever my next literary adventure begins. Your advice, counsel, and calm are so important to me and I will always be grateful. To Peter, Bill, Ree, Lonnie, and the entire team at Thought Leadership Leverage Network, your expertise, strategy, and wisdom will forever be in my mind and heart. You got me through it and made me better than I ever thought I could be, in terms of my reach, vision, and expansive thinking. Thank you for pushing me, thank you for educating me, thank you for elevating me. To Kelly, your creative mind and incredible designs have been a beautiful blessing. Thank you for helping make Stop Settling vivid, memorable, and alive!

And to Kate Purmal, my muse, for going first by writing *The Moonshot Effect* and giving me those three coaching sessions that paved the way for my roadmap. Boy, you are right. We are way ahead of the five-year plan aren't we? Your simultaneous executive level of thinking, coaching, and nurturing continues to wow me. I'm so grateful to you for everything you've done and everything you do. You are such an inspiration.

And finally, thank you to everyone who agreed to sit down for an interview for this book, Mark Sebba (may you now rest in peace), Rosie O'Neill, John Paller, Douglas Conant, Ron Mester, Mara Swan, and Gary Campbell. Your stories and expertise will be forever in my gratitude journal, both literally and figuratively. You are all the epitome of designing a life that works for your situational, relative, and highly prioritized Life Gems. You serve as a blueprint for others to both learn from and follow. By offering up your stories to me, you continued to inspire me and help me connect major and important dots as to how you've created the lives you live. And how those stories and examples may apply to others, as applying them to myself has certainly helped me. Thank you.

INTRODUCTION

I AM HERE to destroy the myth of work-life balance.

I AM HERE to stop you from sprinting inside a hamster wheel that never ends.

I AM HERE to help you become your full authentic self.

Here's the thing: you are complete. When at work. When at home. When in your community. You are the same person in every facet of your life. There are many aspects to life, each varying and changing, and you as a person must go through them all as a dynamic whole. Piecemealing yourself and your time in an attempt to balance the many facets of life disregards the full potential of your happiness, health, and energy.

This notion is the basis of my unique method, mindset, and movement, Stop Settling and this book. Work-life "balance" plagues the modern world with its painted ideal of the superhuman who is able to work a full-time job, be a fantastic friend, always be there for his or her family, donate time to a good cause, and still have time to work out. It's nonsense. Unless you don't sleep, have oodles of money to buy help, or are actually superhuman, you will run yourself ragged trying to "do it all." Most of us are not, and never will be, a Sheryl Sandberg or a Steve Jobs. The reality is that normal people have priorities. They make compromises (mostly unconsciously which is where this book comes in) and devote their time in varied ways. There's no such thing as balance or equilibrium. Just people and the wondrous imperfection that comes with them.

So, isn't it time you accept who you are and decide consciously how you want to spend your time, instead of stressing over how you should be spending your time?

Settle Smart

But before we go any further, let me dispel something. Throw away the notion that settling is always negative. When I say "Stop Settling," I mean stop settling *unconsciously, involuntarily,* and *habitually.* Realize that settling is a noun and a verb. It is a state of being and an action you take. It may mean you're making trade-offs with your time that you may or may not make otherwise. However, when you choose to Settle Smart it will be the most sanity-saving, joy-inducing, productivity-generating habit you have. Thus, for your own sake, it's crucial and imperative that you become self-aware of unconscious habits and *stop settling involuntarily.* Start Settling Smart.

Life events happen to us and from us. Settle Smart is the way through. Events that happen to us include things that are unexpected and often painful and stressful. A loved one gets sick. You lose your home to a natural disaster. The events that happen from us are just as impactful but less of a surprise. You buy a house. You have a child. We actively choose those things. They happen from us. Settle Smart helps you get ahead of the events that happen from you and give you the stability to handle the events that happen to you. Settle Smart helps you move from fight-or-flight mode to thrive mode.

The method is simple when boiled down to its intent and origin. *Stop* is the action you take. *Settling* is positive or negative, situationally and relatively, and totally personal, like a fingerprint. *Smart* is the adjective that describes the healthy, informed, holistic, and integrated approach to the type of Settling you will do when applying the tools, tips, tricks, and traps to avoid offered throughout this book! Be more explicit about the verb *Stop Settling* and the noun *Smart Settling*. The design strategy to Settle Smart is by setting S.M.A.R.T. goals (we'll get into what those look like further into the book).

As this book will ask you to be very personal with yourself, here are a few ground rules:

1. **Be honest.** None of this works if you're lying to yourself about what matters to you. I can't help you if you're in denial.

2. **Leave guilt at the door.** Guilt is just manipulative, emotional warfare. It is habitual, it is learned, and it can be undone. Don't think about what you should be doing because it will make this or that person happy or because it's what your boss expects of you. The only person who can tell you what's important to you is you.

3. **This book is not here to be your therapist. I am not a psychologist.** My decades of networking, managing, mentoring, and developing thousands of individuals and leadership teams, as well as founding my own coaching company, Phoenix[5], have given me a wealth of experience when it comes to helping people master their faceted selves. It was these years of accumulated evidence that birthed the Stop Settling method, mindset, and movement.

If you're open to the possibility that there is no truth to the work-life balance myth, then join me and many others by becoming a Smart Settler!

To make full use of this book, I highly encourage you to take the Stop Settling Quiz (www.phoenix5th.com/stop-settling-quiz) now and again after you finish the book. Move your Settling Spectrum Lever to increase or decrease the amount of time, energy, and passion you give to the five key facets of your life. Live the quality of life that works for YOU! Get off the hamster wheel and watch your productivity and joy increase exponentially.

So, are you ready to wake up?

THE METHOD

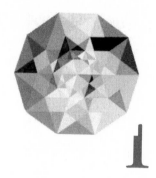

Stop Settling: Turning Carbon into Diamond

HAVE YOU EVER stopped to ask yourself: If I had an endless bucket of money and a magic wand, what's the one thing I would start and the one thing I would stop **today**? If you haven't, do it now. This is how the Stop Settling, Settle Smart journey began for me many years ago.

The work-life balance model is everywhere. There are constant articles from many companies and influential people claiming that they have unlocked the secret to work-life balance and they are now deigning to let you into the club so you may also enjoy the benefits. The urge to achieve work-life balance is intoxicating and coveted. These incredibly successful people, like Sheryl Sandberg and Steve Jobs, are the role models for the modern entrepreneur, yet the life they profess is attainable by maybe a handful of those who try it. According to Arianna Huffington and her sleep study, only 4 percent of humans need only three to four hours of sleep a night.[1] The rest

1 Huffington, Arianna. The Sleep Revolution. Harmony, 2017.

of us get sick and die early when we live that way. We're not all serial entrepreneurs who work all day and ideate all night with an occasional "break" for family and friends. So why are these people our role models? Why are we killing ourselves to achieve something that won't make us happy? This is your one life. To what end are you running?

For the past thirty years of my life, I was running in that hamster wheel. I was the person that sacrificed everything in the pursuit of the mystical nirvana of work-life balance. I worked a full-time career and patted myself on the back when I decided to work from home on Fridays. "You're on your way," I would tell myself. And whenever I made time for my family, I felt like I deserved a parade. "Look how close I am to balancing my work and my life!" I was so sure that the world was a duality. That my career was one half, and everything else—my "life"—was always out of balance. And once I achieved that balance, once I had it all by being my all and of course doing it all, then all my problems would disappear. The guilt I felt for not being with my kids as much, for not working out, for being absent in my community, would just melt away. So I did everything to reach that balance. I bought the bullshit.

And I did it. I got there. I achieved the "balance." I had run my life like a start-up and arrived at that imagined state. My first marriage was failing, friendships were few and far between, and I spent no time on my own health or welfare. But I was positive I had reached the "balance."

And as I stood for that brief moment, in the middle of that teeter-totter, I felt … tired. Then the moment passed and I, in my little proverbial hamster wheel, rolled to one side and the process started all over again. I never realized that I was out of alignment. I simply thought I was Type A, an overachiever, and at times a workaholic.

I used to say, as if it were some pride-based mantra, "I thrive in chaos" and so I did ... or did I? And, guess what people, I *am* a Type A overachiever who is a bit of a workaholic but there's more to my life than that.

Even if you aren't struggling with the extremes, you still feel something is missing or there's never enough time. That same feeling is still apparent. This is why I created the Stop Settling method (quiz and spectrum), which grew into a mindset, then ultimately into a movement for myself, family, friends, community, and now, the world.

Perhaps my biggest issue with work-life balance is that it separates work and life. As if work is an isolated world unto itself. A world in which you may be playing a part, wearing a mask, or even reinventing yourself. As if it's an identity that exists outside of your real life. *But life is the wrapper around all of it.*

This is how it all began. Stop Settling, Phoenix[5], the Gem in the logo, the colors related to the facets—all of it. After I consciously decided to become a corporate defector, I began seriously thinking about my own company and Stop Settling. What did I want it to stand for? What was the message I wanted to convey?

The Stop Settling "ideal" will look different for each person. There is no specific goal to reach here except for the goals and values you set for yourself. The Stop Settling Quiz (please take it now if you haven't yet: www.phoenix5th.com/stop-settling-quiz) and the Life Gem you receive at the end of the quiz are split up into five different facets: Career, Generations (your family), Circle (your friendships), Society (your community), and Vitality (your well-being). Each facet has a unique color and they all fit together to make up your complete life, hence the name Life Gem. It's the visual representation of how you scale in the five facets. The scale the quiz uses stretches from

Always Settling to Never Settling to help you rate the importance that each of these facets holds for you. They will not all be equal. You will need to consciously choose how much time and effort you want to put into each one.

People who fully embrace Stop Settling and start Settling Smart prioritize where they spend their time based on what they want. They spend their time with things and people that make them feel happy and fulfilled, no apologies made or guilt felt for their decision. We're all unique. And despite the judging ego, there's no right or wrong, good or bad in this case. Stop Settling is a joy-inducing, productivity-generating, self-actualizing tool and practice that will help you achieve the things *you actually want to do* without having to run yourself ragged trying to "do it all."

You will be your all by not doing it all.

The Birth of Stop Settling

The major "aha" moment came around the end of my time in the corporate world. I had refined a time and motion type of question to help determine how people spend their time and energy. I used to ask, and still ask, my teams, boards, and leadership coaching clients, friends, and family (when they tolerate me), "If you had an endless bucket of money and a magic wand, what is the one thing you would start and one thing you would stop, today?" I began to realize that one too many of my coworkers responded with "Do you mean personal or professional?" "Do you mean work or life?" It felt so wrong to hear those questions asked, but for the longest time I didn't know why. Then it hit me. If we decouple the way we live based on work or life, we'll never get off the hamster wheel.

The colors of the Gem, including your personal Life Gem, display the many facets of life while indicating a constant transitive phase: one in which we're always evolving and changing. And that's what makes us beautiful and interesting. That's when I happened upon the top-down image of a diamond. It was perfect. All these colors playing inside of an object that was once a hunk of coal. And depending on how you looked at it, the colors shifted. That was it.

The specific colors and the facets were inspired by gems and stones that not only matched the color but conveyed the meaning behind each facet. Ultimately, I decided on the following:

- Career
  - Gold/ Citrine (Yellow)
  - Meaning: wealth, status, achievement
- Generations (Family)
  - Bloodstone (Red)
  - Meaning: safety, survival, nourishment
- Circle (Friendships)
  - Aquamarine (Blue)
  - Meaning: friendship, patience, loyalty
- Society (Community)
  - Lapis Lazuli (Purple)
  - Meaning: truth, self-expression, communication
- Vitality (Well-being)
  - Jade (Green)
  - Meaning: health, renewal, healing

The Method

These colors still represent the facets today. When you take the quiz, the colors in the Gem align with how much of your time you dedicate to each facet, and your primary trait(s) are also in the colors that represent who you are.

For us to truly realize who we are, beyond who we were born to be, there is a ton of life stuff thrown our way. At times things are wildly complex and other times as simple and crystal clear as the smell of a rose you stop to actually sniff, the way you feel instant unconditional love with your newborn baby, the spark between you and a loved one or friend, the passion you run on at work when you're in the zone, the sheer and utter joy of helping someone out, or the natural high of completing a workout. All of this stuff is what makes life truly successful. And, whether you are seeing these quiz takers gems in full color or greyscale, check out the aggregate findings from over 1,000 responses as to their current vs. desired quality of life:

Quiz Scale	Label	Scoring
1	**Always Settling**	0-19
2	**Frequently Settling**	20-39
3	**Neutral**	40-59
4	**Infrequently Settling**	60-79
5	**Never Settling**	80-100

On average, most people are ranking their Current Life Gems in Frequently Settling and Neutral. And in general, people aspire to be in Neutral and Infrequently Settling in their Desired Life Gems. This is just the beginning and a snapshot of early quiz takers from the first six months of launching the quiz!

My Stop Settling Manifesto says, "Stop Settling is an intuitive, simple, and rapid approach for asking and answering the question necessary to maintain momentum within the unique edges of our defined whole." This is just my fancy way of saying it really doesn't take that long to wake up and live your life consciously. Your life is your choice. Stop Settling is here to empower individuals to make choices knowingly, consciously, and flexibly throughout life's ups and downs, situationally and relatively. To help you on this journey, I have divided this book into three major phases which, unlike other systems approaches, is designed to be followed in sequence. For those of you that like to rush to the end, knock yourself out, but the punchline won't make sense without the learnings along the way. These phases are: 1) The Method, 2) The Mindset, and 3) The Movement.

The Method

The Stop Settling spectrum helps you prioritize and de-prioritize what's most important to you, right now and in your future.

The quiz will ask you to rate yourself on a scale from Always Settling to Never Settling and provide you with your Current and Desired Life Gems. The combinations and permutations that make up your Life Gems are never all or nothing. The only time that works is in Texas hold 'em. The various gem patterns that emerge simulate a kaleidoscope for one's life.

What are you aspiring toward? How will you get there? It all starts with knowing. Be conscious. Where are you spending the most time for the most enjoyment? What is your Return on Enjoyment (ROE)? Identifying this will help you build your Life Gem with purpose, focus, and clarity. This won't happen by default.

The Stop Settling five-point scale and five-question quiz is designed to answer the giant and seemingly impossible question, "What is it that I really want for the quality of my complete life?" This includes the five facets that Stop Settling operates on:

Career

Career is sometimes the classic working to live or living to work. Your daily nine to five (or longer for many of us), office-sitting, and/or standing, back-to-back-meetings life. This category includes your job, perhaps even your own start-up company, and any passionate work aspirations you may have within this realm. For many, our identity and self-worth are wrapped up here, tightly.

Generations

Generations is your family. Parents, kids, grandparents, in-laws, etc. Anyone in your life who is or whom you consider close family. This doesn't really include your second cousin twice removed that lives in an obscure town that you only chitchat with during the five-year family reunion. And if it does, you really need to take the quiz! This is for the family whom you interact with regularly enough that they have a significant impact on your time.

Circle

Circle is your friends. The people in your life with whom you choose to grab coffee or dinner. The people you go to when you want to have fun! The ones you call when the two aforementioned facets are driving you up the wall. You know, real friends. For some of us, blood is not thicker than water, and perhaps some of your closest friends you consider family. YOU define this; no one else gets to.

Society

Society is your community. This may be your church, book club, where you volunteer, the local farmers market to which you contribute. Anything where you interact with your community at large.

Vitality

Vitality is your health and wellness. And while it includes your physical health, it's not limited to that. This signifies the things you do to keep your sanity, avoid burnout, and reconnect with your personal bliss. This category is about physical activities like running and yoga as well as activities like hobbies, meditation, and passion projects.

Why Did I Choose This Scale?

Always and *Never* are extreme and almost impossible to achieve without major damage, in particular to oneself, let alone to everyone else. I don't recommend them because they're so extreme. This can be a difficult concept to adopt, especially in today's world, where you're constantly being told to give it your all while being your all!

To illustrate, recently during a keynote, I had the audience take the quiz. Most of the participants resonated with the quiz and said it was a gratifying success overall. One woman, however, came up to me after my talk and said, "This is so great for everyone but me. I never settle in any facet of any kind, *ever*." I don't believe her. It's not a sustainable or healthy way to live. I would challenge that even Oprah—with all her endless means and support—settles in some of the five domains.

If you're living your life in a way that you're Never Settling in any facet, you're a hamster in a wheel. Unless you completely throw out three of the five domains, then sure. But for us mere mortals, the five facets are part of us. No matter how you spin the wheel, something will be traded off. It will never be stagnant. I don't buy it, whether you're telling yourself or someone is telling you. IF this were for robots, this would be a very different conversation. HAL 9000 would ace the quiz. But a perfect score is more akin to work-life balance than to Smart Settling.

The Spectrum:

- *Always Settling* means that this is the lowest priority for you. You aren't/don't want to put effort into it. It just doesn't interest you. If you're Always Settling in multiple facets, you've most likely completely settled unconsciously or involuntarily, and you feel stuck.
- *Frequently Settling* means that it's a low priority for you. When you have to do something under this facet, you push it down on your list, consciously or otherwise. You have more important things to prioritize.
- *Neutral* means you're good where you are. It's smooth sailing.
- *Infrequently Settling* means that it's a high priority for you. You're in this facet a lot. Whether or not you want to be is a different matter! It's taking up a big chunk of your time and occupying a large part of your life.
- *Never Settling* means it's the highest priority for you. This is where you spend the majority of your time and life. You rarely ever say no to an opportunity or task here. When in this mode you're hyper-driven, mowing things down and relentless in your pursuits. If too many facets are here, you may be running out of steam. There's a limit.

Who Are You?

At the end of the quiz, you will be given your primary trait(s). These will illustrate the facet(s) that you prioritize the highest.

- *Careerist* is for those of you who prioritize the Career facet. If you're a Careerist then doing your job, working, and spending time in your career fills you with purpose, helps you define your identity, and makes you feel like you're contributing. Oh, and you probably like money. Not for nothing; many of us simply need to work as providers. This goes beyond that. You've probably been heard excitedly declaring, "Show me the money!"

- *Family First* is for those of you who prioritize the Generations facet. Family Firsters give and receive constantly. When you're with family (even if they're not blood-related) you fill with joy and love and thrive off the connection. You live the phrase, "Charity starts at home."

- *Social* is for those of you who prioritize the Circle facet. If you're Social, you are fun, engaging, and thrive off being around your friends. If you have regular group outings to restaurants, host book clubs, attend reunions, etc. with your friends, this is your trait. They just "get you."

- *Activist* is for those of you who prioritize the Society facet. You love to give back. You're a change agent who wants to leave your mark on this world while improving social consciousness. "Volunteering" is probably your favorite word, let alone verb.

- *Green Machine* is for those of you who prioritize the Vitality facet. Your body is your temple. You understand that you only get one body, one mind, and one life, so you cherish and take care of them. You may be heard saying, "You are what you eat."

After taking the quiz, you will face one of two scenarios: the first being the excitement of seeing a dynamic visual representation of your current and future priorities and the thrill of beginning to work toward your holistic life, the second being either shock or disappointment by your Current Life Gem. It's okay. That's why you have your Desired Life Gem to work toward.

Most likely, you've been walking through life asleep and on autopilot (no offense meant, most of us are). But you're now taking the steps to wake up and stay awake, recognizing the power of things like choice, options, and the ability to design your life. You're moving out of default and into the power of design-thinking your life. We map most things out, even if it's just going out for a walk in a new city. There's always an app for that. Why not our one life? Let's jump into the driver's seat.

The Mindset

The Mindset is the shift dynamic of believing that it's not just okay but mandatory to ask oneself what is it that you really want for *your* quality of life. It's moving past what you think you should want or what you think others want or expect from you. The Mindset trades the habits of work-life balance (the only way to be your all is to do it all) in favor of thriving in your dynamic multifaceted self.

To fully immerse yourself in the Mindset, follow these steps:

The Method

1. Take five.

   a. Slow down for five minutes and clear your mind. Try an exercise like this one: While sitting, plant your feet firmly on the ground and place your hands with palms up on top of your knees. Straighten your back, close your eyes, and take three deep breaths. With each exhale, let the cares, worries, and general noise leave your brain. Allow yourself to stay in this meditative state, focusing on your breathing, for about five minutes.

   b. Take the Stop Settling Quiz (if you haven't yet) without any "shoulds." Simply answer the questions as honestly as you are able.

   c. Review your results, really taking in what they say to you about the changes you need to make to achieve your Desired Quality of Life.

   d. Start implementing the changes! Share them with a spouse, friend, or whomever you trust to encourage you and kick you back into gear when you falter. Set up for success incrementally, not in wide-sweeping changes. No Big Bang here. Go for a phased approach.

2. Shift your dynamic up (or back!) along the spectrum.

   a. Focus on the changes from step one and where you have to move to achieve your goals. It's healthy and productive to shift forward to settle less and shift backward to settle more.

   b. Read this book (you're off to a good start!) cover to cover. Go back to the tools, tips, and takeaways at the end of each chapter from time to time to refresh your memory.

c. You can also look up my YouTube videos, listen to my podcasts, read my blog, or come see me speak! I have developed many mediums to help people be their best selves and further their journey toward the Stop Settling mindset. All you need to do is look!

3. Reassess, adjust, rinse, and repeat.

a. Retake the quiz as your life changes situationally and relatively.

b. Share the quiz with loved ones, friends, and coworkers. It makes for great dinner conversation and fosters deeper understanding, appreciation, and accountability both to and from one another.

c. Celebrate the victories! It's not easy to understand what you truly want and it's even harder to actualize your goals. When you reach your goals, take some time to pat yourself on the back and recognize a job well done.

4. Be accountable.

a. This one is pretty self-explanatory. Commit to your changes! You, along with others who are key in your life, ensure the change is lasting and understood for yourself.

b. You will have bad days. You will have times when you feel like you've failed. That's okay! Give yourself a break. Pick yourself up and take each day at a time. Remember why you pulled your settle lever up or back and get back on track!

c. Stop Settling is designed to start with you. You will make the shift and you will own the successes and failures. It's a choice. Be aware when you're making this choice, even when it might not be active or conscious. And for those of you recovering control freaks (hear, hear!), accept that there are limits to what you control. But you do have a choice. More honestly, you only have the power of choice, whether you make it actively, passively, or seemingly not at all.

The Movement

The Movement is knowing how to answer the question. Trying to answer selfishly and completely without knowing yourself is hard, but it's infinitely harder to go for it consciously. Act or you're not part of the movement. The Method and the Mindset are there as tools; the Movement is up to you.

The Movement may present itself in various ways. Let me give you an example. This past Mother's Day, my fourteen-year-old, who normally avoids and otherwise attempts to ignore me altogether, wrote me a beautiful card. She wrote,

Thank you, Mom, for going for your dream. It's so cool to watch you accomplish things right in front of us. It gives me hope for my own life.

Imagine my absolute and astonished delight that my choices have had such a positive effect on my daughter. She sees her mother making choices and not apologizing for them. By living Stop Settling the Movement, by doing what I *love*, what brings me joy and feeds my soul, what serves my purpose in life, is helping her learn how to operate her human system with authenticity. I call this mode of operating ABHOS, Authenticity Based Human Operating System.

Of all the lessons I'm able to teach her and the love I'm able to give her, the best way for me to set her up for a successful, happy, and independent adult life is to lead by example. Sometimes I settle less and sometimes I settle more. And that, my friends, is Settling Smart!

Two truths and no lie:

1. Harmony beats balance every time.
2. And-versus-or thinking will set you free when brainstorming.

In Silicon Valley we are masters of building on others' thoughts, experiences, and visions, of building in collaboration when working in teams, by saying "yes and." Unfortunately, in our multidimensional and faceted lives this may be a trap to avoid. We must learn when to say "I will do this" or "I will do that." It is veritably impossible to always achieve "yes and" even if we find ourselves always saying "yes and!"

Takeaways—Fact Versus Fiction:

Throughout this book, at the end of each chapter you will notice that there's a sum-up of key takeaways, trips, and tricks, as well as traps to avoid. These are called *Takeaways Brought to You by Fact Versus Fiction*. Fact versus Fiction is one of my favorite tools in my coaching toolkit and we will get into it later in the book.

These sections will help you navigate most common pitfalls to avoid and stop you from expending a ton of precious emotional and mental headspace on things that are simply not true. Instead, I guide you through how to quickly ensure that you're actually emoting in response to things that are fact-based. This will save you tons of time and energy and keep you out of the giant traps that are negative beliefs and perceptions.

You with me? Let's go!

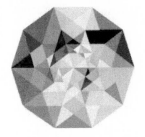

2

CAREER

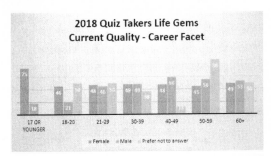

Here, depending on the age range and gender, we start to see larger jumps from Current to Desired Life Gems. On average, people are taking their Settling Spectrum levers and pulling back into healthy and positive settling (settling more) as well as pushing hard towards acceleration in one's career and Never Settling. We also see some women pushing harder toward less Frequently Settling as they age. While some men and women are holding steady, happy with where they are now and in their Desired Life Gems. And even some quiz takers, both men and women, wanting to settle less as they reach the upper age bracket of 60+. This could indicate a 2nd or 3rd career, passion work, or even retiring and staying on part-time.

What is Career?

THE CAREER FACET is all about making an impact, being a contributor, creating stability in your and possibly your family's life, and making money. I know that last one may make people uncomfortable, but it's the truth. Your career is about making money, which in turn gives you freedom to live your life as you desire. Don't give money any more weight than it already carries. It's nothing more than the power to choose in paper form.

My best friend has been working in the same position, in the same company, which has not treated her well, for eleven years. She's finally realizing what she has earned and what she is worth. And in taking her next career leap, she has finally stopped settling.

Chasing the dollar has nothing to do with chasing the dream.

Let's be honest. For most of us, whether we like it or not, our work—our career—takes up most of our time. If we work in an office, we're there for about eight hours a day, not including our commute. If we work at home, we're in front of our computers or in our home offices for just as long if not longer. It's easy to let work take over our whole Gem, and for some of us that's not a problem while others want to be able to step back a little.

A badass and a former board member, Shanti, said it so well when I was researching both the book and the concept of Stop Settling. It is her nonapologetic way of living her life as an executive, attorney, founder, CEO, member of multiple boards, wife, and mother. She said:

> Look, sometimes I make the kids' soccer games and sometimes I don't. Do I make every practice? Absolutely not. Major games? Yes, whenever possible. And if I'm unable, and my husband is able to go, I don't feel bad about it or do the guilt

thing. Here's the deal. We make trade-offs. Mine are conscious. I love what I do in all aspects of my life, and my kids and my family get that. They don't feel as if they are less important to me because I am explicit about how I am willing to spend my time and my reasoning behind my decisions. They know I am all in whenever I do anything. That thing I'm focused on gets all of me. And I wouldn't trade that!

Her unabashed and honest way of living her life realized the idea I had been kicking around in my head for years. She didn't hold her passions or time to anyone's standards but her own. She knew what she wanted and how she was going to get it. She accepted that it meant that other facets of her life may be given less time. And with that knowledge, she still *consciously* made that decision.

That's what it's all about. Be honest with yourself and those around you about what you want. You are beholden to no one but yourself! Even the big players like Jeff Bezos, CEO of Amazon, and Kristin Lemkau, CMO of JP Morgan Chase, are shifting away from work-life balance toward work-life integration.[2]

It's not about balance, it's about harmony.

Is Your Leader the Right Fit for You?

As my amazing former colleague Mara Swan, executive vice president of Global Strategy and Talent at ManpowerGroup, said to me during our interview:

It's who you work for that matters, not the company. Do you

---

2 Lebowitz, Shana. "Top Execs in Banking, Retail, and Tech Are Saying They Don't Practice Work-Life Balance— Because They Found Something Better." Business Insider, Business Insider, 30 June 2018, www.businessinsider.com/jp-morgan-chase-cmo-other-execs-value-work-life-integration-2018-6.

have a leader, executive or manager that is smart, pushing you, and promoting you organizationally? It matters. I underestimated that. You want a leader that pushes the envelope even when it's not in your wheelhouse and forces you to lean into discomfort, or it's not the best job for you to take. Believe in yourself! Belief in yourself is where things start.[3]

Look for a company that values learning as much as working. Nowadays, employees spend too much time working versus learning. Having a leader that pays attention to your learning and growth helps you achieve goals based on insights from the assessment while being a more productive and happier employee.

Lots of activity is not necessarily indicative of results. The real question is, what direction are we going in and how do I adjust?

Career in My Life

Is it ironic that on June 30, 2018, as I'm writing this book and in the throes of spending a fortune of my time, emotional investment, cold hard cash, and even a piece of my *much* needed vacation time with my family and friends to pour out of my head and into this book my ideas and, ultimately, my soul? I think not. But I am consciously choosing to take a portion of my time that is meant for the Vitality facet and put it into the Career facet, which is where I categorize this book, since "universal" isn't a facet. It's so important to me and I know my family understands. I'm not "balancing" my family and writing time on the vacation. I'm choosing to spend a little less time with my family and more on my passion in writing this book,

---

3 Swan, Mara. Personal interview. 26 Jun. 2018.

because it's important to me. Work-life balance is a *fraud*. And it was my relationship with Career that woke me up to that.

So, perhaps to truly understand this facet, we need to take a trip down memory lane.

The Career facet has played a role in my life since the age of eight when I set up a pretend office in our den, on an old card table, with our old-school rotary telephone. My "office" was filled with index cards, pens and pencils, a calculator, and other supplies. I would spend hours playing. Where this came from, I have no friggin' idea.

But I loved it.

I wanted to be that important "office lady," with the big office and file cabinets. This was a strange aspiration given that my father was a dentist and my mother was a stay-at-home mom.

As an enterprising teen, wanting both the independence and freedom that money provides, I started babysitting at the age of thirteen for an incredible family who eventually grew into my second family. They became my haven and destination of choice for the next six years of my life as my mother's undiagnosed bipolar disorder permeated our home. Blending the spirit of giving back and commerce from the start, I took care of a special-needs six-month-old, Curtie, and his two incredible older brothers, who were three and five at the time. As Curt grew, he was also diagnosed with Type 1 diabetes. I worked hand in hand with his mama (Love You, Deb!) and father to take care of and support this little guy. I spent years working with this family and loving every minute of it. I was able to earn enough money to have the freedom and independence I craved, and most importantly, I was able to help and make an impact in these kids' lives. Giving back simply felt right. It's a theme that continues to weave throughout my life.

Later, as I matured, I realized my other passion: ballet. It was my salvation and my recharge zone. When I danced, my cup would fill with energy. And I used that energy to continue to help others and work on myself as a leader.

As my colorful college experience was coming to a close, my sister died. I was twenty, almost twenty-one. And I became a full-blown, completely functioning, workaholic.

The drive and passion that I applied to all of my endeavors, from teaching aerobics to being the weekend manager at a health club, propelled my fight-or-flight reaction. I was both running from and toward my dysfunctional family.

Next, I somehow fell into a world that up until that point I didn't know existed: staffing. For those of you unfamiliar with this multi-trillion-dollar global industry, think of things like temporary and contract labor with millions (and growing) independent contractors and freelancers. This is also known as the nonemployee workforce: all the people not being paid on a W2 by a corporation or firm directly. This is such a huge and growing component of how work gets done in the modern world that for those of us wanting to make a difference in people's lives while making a good living, it was perfect for me. So much so that it lasted more than twenty-one years.

As I became a recruiter, I was so proud of putting people to work. My roommate and best friend to this day would roll her eyes at me as I'd get excited to go back to work after a long, sometimes ten- or eleven-hour day.

But I was having so much fun.

I loved my candidates and took pride in placing them in the optimum job at the company that was the best fit. I wanted to help these people succeed and I became their career coach, confidant, and agent. My intuition went way beyond the company's practical and formulaic approach to placements. I simply knew when there was a match. I had, or developed, a sixth sense as to who would fit where, when, and how. Often to the astonishment of my coworkers and boss. I had, within a snapshot of time, placed sixty different people who were all working with me as their liaison to ensure fit, success, and future raises and extensions of work. I was damn proud of that.

I would continue this way. I did have a four-year "heart job" at a nonprofit in between that was more from my heart than our family wallet, but for the most part, I continued up the corporate ladder, taking calculated risks along the way.

That is until I hit my head on the glass ceiling, hard.

Luckily, not as hard as Arianna Huffington hit hers on a glass coffee table. The wake-up calls as to what is settling and what is not started out as a whisper and ended with a pit in my stomach. I would make moves up and out of each corporation that either didn't treat people right, when hypocrisy set in, or when I was expected to step on or sleep with someone to get ahead. It felt like it was always my time to go. I just couldn't achieve that balance.

Enter my fantastic boss, mentor, and Leader of His Life, who effectively blew up the "balance" ideal in exchange for integration. And apologies in advance, Ron, but I may embarrass you a little bit here.

In my eyes, Ron seemed to have it all, in the most sustainable and high-integrity way. He would eventually become part of my inspiration for ABHOS, the Authenticity Based Human Operating System. It's an operating system for people that still maintains individuality yet is adjoined by the common core of authenticity. I always saw five major facets to Ron:

The Man	The Husband	The Father	The Management consultant	The Serial entrepreneur/CEO
Business-minded	Married Harvard Law sweetheart	Always there	Did it his way	2–3 start-ups with successes and some failures
Kind-hearted	Proud of family	Always present	Contrarian success	1 with a Big-F Failure (I'll explain what that is in a minute)
Intelligent	Supportive	Instiller of female confidence	Challenged status quo	
	Healthy ego	Fantastic listener		
		Hilarious storyteller		

The Post-it Strategy

I was about a year into my career working for Ron at Staffing Industry Analysts I'd entered in an individual contributor position and worked very hard for a year. Ron had pushed me and stretched me, and it was all good. When it was time for the annual review, he had a plan for promotion and raises that I didn't anticipate. We were at an airport waiting for a flight when Ron decided to discuss my promotion and raise. Via Post-it notes.

He had me write down, on a Post-it, what I felt was an appropriate salary, and he wrote down his number on his Post-it. This way I knew his offer was genuine and uninfluenced by my number. We revealed our numbers to each other and, of course, my number was lower. At that point, I thought I'd blown it. I came in too low and now I was stuck with it. But, Ron grabbed my number out of my hand with a

"Give me that!" He told me he'd thought long and hard about the number and felt that this was the amount I deserved.

The philosophy behind this technique is simple: "Compensation shouldn't be a negotiation because we're both on the same side."

Lead Don't Tell

In my efforts to achieve balance, I told Ron that I needed to be out of the office by 4:30 p.m. every day so that I could be with my daughters. Being the supportive boss that he was, he said absolutely. But more than giving me permission, he would hold me accountable. At 4:25pm, if I still had not started to pack up to leave, he would stick his head in my office and remind me, "It's 4:25!" He would literally kick me out! Of my own office! But I was grateful. He showed me that there's a way to integrate the various aspects of your life in a way that you can do what you want to do. Sometimes, you just need a little practice.

In his words:

The best employees are the people who are passionate about their work and are performing the best, have the hardest time knowing when to create that integration. It is integration and not so much balance. People who are ambitious have a hard time drawing lines and figuring out how to integrate. As a general rule, people don't believe CEOs when they say that they want their employees to spend time with their families or that they care about their personal lives. They think the CEO is just reading lines but doesn't actually care. So, I felt the only way I could show people that I meant what I said was by demonstrating it.[4]

4 Mester, Ron. Personal interview. 3 Jul. 2018.

Career in Life Today

When you look at my daily schedule it looks like a trafficking schedule at a TV station, according to my beloved husband. It's filled with what's important to me along my Settle Smart guidelines. A current typical day will look like: drive fourteen- year-old to school; walk dogs; coach three clients; attend a writer's bootcamp to finish this book; make dinner—or not; eat with hubby, fourteen-year-old, and a few of her friends—or not; and finally, relax by watching or reading something before sleep.

This is my idea of a super-full yet integrated day. Yours will probably look completely different. The point is that it should make you excited, happy, and fulfilled.

The Lessons

Embrace Failure

Failure is a natural part of life and it's definitely a natural part of business. You will try things and you will fail. Ron was the one who taught me about Big Fs and Little Fs.

He saw that people, in general, were terrified of failure. They think about avoiding failure. And while he understands the natural aversion, he disagrees with it. Ron wants people to embrace failure. It's unavoidable so you may as well accept it. If you really want to make change and you really want to make an impact, that means you're going to be trying something new. Every venture simply won't work, which means you will fail. Big F and Little Fs are Ron's way of differentiating between failures.

Big Fs are big failures. Start-ups going under. Losing a major client. Little Fs are small failures. Sales proposal gone wrong. Failure in executing a project on deadline. You'll experience both in your life, but the point is to have few Big Fs and lots of Little Fs. Having lots of Little Fs means you're innovating. You're trying new things. But most importantly, you're getting comfortable with failure.

Set Yourself Up for Success—With Failure

The more you innovate, the more you try new things, the more you learn. This learning builds up a wealth of experience and knowledge. You are building up an arsenal of tips, tricks, tools, and how-tos for a large variety of situations. That way when it comes time to take a big risk (that can result in a Big F), you have the wisdom to navigate potential pitfalls and problems that you know don't work because you have tested so many scenarios! Not only that, but if the big risk results in a Big F, failing doesn't tear you down in the same way.

Dealing with Big Fs

Dealing with Big Fs is a lot harder than dealing with the little ones. These failures often come with some type of monetary or pride hit. Getting past them, however, is not so much different than dealing with Little Fs. If something small goes wrong, you assess the situation, see where things went wrong, reformat the plan, and push forward. With a Big F, the process is the same save for one very important step in the beginning: give yourself a little time. Give yourself a quick breather: five minutes, one day, one week— you determine how long you need—to feel the pain and deal with it. Once you have given yourself adequate time to internalize the failure, then and only then should you proceed to the same steps as for the Little F.

60/30/10 Your Life

The 60/30/10 idea was adapted from fortune company CEO Brad Smith's method, along with a bunch of other concepts and frames I'd been using before I even knew they were designs. In his version, Smith talks about how his leadership team operates by focusing 60 percent of its time on day-to-day tasks; 30 percent in adrenaline-junkie mode, looking for what's hot and what's next; and 10 percent on diving for sunken treasure, that is, working toward a big, wild, audacious goal that is game-changing and/or market-making.

I love this design and find it extends beyond the realm of business. In fact, as is the theme of this book, it applies beautifully to the other facets of your life. But let's first explore what it looks like at work and in business.

Being a 60/30/10 Leader

First off, let me give you my definition of leader. It's more than just someone who is put in charge of people. A true leader extends past career and work. So for those of you content with not being leaders at work, stay with me! Leaders are people who are in charge of their lives and lead them with conscious confidence so that others want to follow. They may manage people at their work, be parents inspiring their children to live better lives, be active in their community and bringing awareness to important issues, or just simply be in the driver's seat of their life. Leaders wear more than business suits. (We'll cover more about being the leader of your life in Chapter 7.)

60-percent Horizon

This is where the day-to-day operational focus areas live that you must address, hold accountable to, and eventually perform yourself. The 60-percent horizon should feel slightly rote and maybe even a bit boring (especially for us ADD types—squirrel?) yet also provide a sense of comfort in routine. This may include emails, phone calls, meetings ad nauseam, client pitches, etc. Most of your time will be spent in this horizon.

30-percent Horizon

This horizon is where you push boundaries and edge out of your comfort zone. This percentile is where you explore new products, services, and anything that will bring something fresh and new to shake up the company in a healthy way. These products and services are typically complementary to what you already do really well as an organization. If you really want to go the extra mile here, try taking apart and rebuilding products and services you already have so that they function better or bring in more revenue.

10-percent Horizon

This is reserved for the giant, stomach-wrenching, sweat-inducing leaps. This is where you start putting into action one of those wild ideas that have been floating around in your mind or that you hastily scribbled down on a bar napkin. This horizon will unceremoniously shove you out of your comfort zone. But it's just tough love. This is so you can innovate something completely new. Some companies call this a moonshot. Time, place, and plan are key for you to pull it off if you're going to spend 10 percent of your time, energy, and resources exploring this lofty goal. Stay focused and embrace the leap.

You can achieve amazing things in this category. For one of my clients, the CEO of HireTalent, this became the birth of the diversity and inclusion movement called Consciously Unbiased (Go, Ash!).

60/30/10 Outside of Work

So, what does this look like in your everyday life?

The 60-percent horizon is all the chores that need to get done in our daily lives. The dishes, laundry, driving kids to and from school and activities, walking the dogs, brushing teeth, etc.

The 30-percent horizon here is more like redecorating a room, going from no dishwasher to having a dishwasher, taking time for yourself to meditate, doing yoga, going to a retreat, or reading a book. It's about doing something mindful that's not every day. (Washing windows goes here as well as it's not every day but it's still about taking care of what you have.)

The 10-percent horizon is deciding to run a marathon for the first time. You're unprepared and unathletic, preferring the comforts of your couch to that of uncomfortable sweating and panting. But either because you want to live a bit healthier or because you thought it would be a good idea to accept the challenge from a friend, you need to prepare. So you create a training regime and complete your moonshot. This category also could include buying and/or building a home or hosting an exchange student for a year so your kids can learn French.

There's something important to remember when you're applying the 60/30/10 method to your whole life. Do not try and convert the 10-percent horizon into the 60-percent horizon. It's unsustainable.

You will run out of time, resources, and energy very quickly. These horizons build on each other. The 60 percent gives you the stability to branch out into the 30 percent. The 30 percent helps you narrow down the projects that are worth your time in the 10 percent.

Keep these horizons as they are or you will burn yourself out and ultimately feel unstable at the end of the day.

It's all about mapping out your life by design. Does your 60/30/10 fit your desired life gem? Track your 60/30/10 at work and at home and find out! Give it two weeks or a month. Soon, you will see you're robbing from Peter's 30 and 10 percents to pay Paul's 60 percent. Stop that! Most likely, it's involuntary settling that's taken over here. Be conscious about where you are and master your faceted self!

Takeaways Brought to You by Fact Versus Fiction:

Fiction #1: If I wear a mask at work, no one will know that I'm an impostor and I'll be able to keep it all together.

Fact #1: We all suffer from impostor syndrome at some point in our lives; for some of us, it's on the daily. If Meryl Streep, Sheryl Sandberg, and even the incredible author Neil Gaiman suffer from this, we can too! You might also check out Amy Cuddy's viral "fake it till you make it" Ted Talk on body language.[5] Her antidote is power posing. I've tried it, and it works.

Fiction #2.1: It's okay to walk the walk and not talk the talk.

Fiction #2.2: It's okay to talk the talk and not walk the walk.

---

5 Cuddy, Amy. "Your body language may shape who you are." YouTube, uploaded by TED, 1 October 2012, https://www.youtube.com/watch?v=Ks-_Mh1QhMc.

Fact #2: Lead by example. It will never fail you, your team, your family, or anyone for that matter.

Fiction #3: If I have a Big F, I'm done.

Fact #3: There are Little Fs and Big Fs in Failure. Know the difference and learn to celebrate the Little Fs. Practice makes permanent!

Fiction #4: When leading a company, it's cool to hang on tight to the reins and never let anyone else take over. You're the captain, you must go down with the ship.

Fact #4.1: Remember Blockbuster? They may have been taken out practically overnight by Netflix; however, they had an incredible run and practically made their own market before the next wave crashed over them toward the digital and streaming future. They weren't idiots. They also weren't futurists. Some things run their course.

Fact #4.2: You're not always the best person to lead your company. Sometimes things outgrow you and sometimes you outgrow things.

Fact #4.3: We are not on the Titanic, people.

Fiction #5: If I cram everything in at work and get tons of stuff done, I'll be hyper-productive and known as a go-to person.

Fact #5: You must move toward the 60/30/10 approach. Place 60 percent of your time, energy, and efforts into the day-to-day tactics and routines at work and home. Use 30 percent of your time, energy, and efforts to evolve into what's best and next for your products, services, kids' growing needs and your own! Be a little bit of a risk-taker even if it's not in your nature, and spend a little time throwing a bit of caution to the wind, as long as it's thinking and actions which consider both the risks and the rewards, and that work for you (not for your boss, not for your neighbor, not for your mentor, for you)!

(Note: If you work within a team, have a great marital partnership, or sit on the volunteer board of the PTA, you might need to loosen up a bit and come toward the middle in this 30-percent realm.) And finally, the 10-percent horizon. This is your deep dive into the unknown, your big hairy audacious goal, your moonshot. Nothing ventured, nothing gained. Don't risk the farm but do go for it! If you spend just a little bit of your precious life in this mode, you will be able to say that this journey had some incredible high notes. This horizon is not for the faint of heart; however, much like me writing this book, you will never know if you do not try.

Fiction #6: Only a Yoda voice saying, "Do or do not, there is no try" is effective in team meetings or at the dinner table.

Fact #6: It's annoying! Just use your regular voice.

Fact #6.1: I'm saving you a lot of embarrassment.

3

GENERATIONS

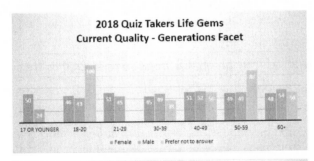

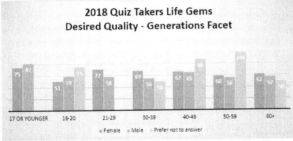

On average, when looking at the Generations facet, patterns emerge. We start to see a lot of Neutral answers on the Current Life Gem with most people desiring Infrequently Settling. There are a few interesting results here, in that some of the young people, wanted to go from Never Settling to Infrequently Settling, while others went from Neutral to Infrequently Settling. We also start to notice women in this facet moving their Settling Spectrum levers towards the upper end of Infrequently Settling than men, as age increases.

THE GENERATIONS FACET is all about warmth. It's about the joy, comfort, safety, and unconditional love that family ideally provides. This facet, more than perhaps any of the others, is extremely personal, not only in experience but also in definition.

Blood is Not Always Thicker Than Water

The definition of family according to the Oxford English Dictionary is "A group of people related by blood or marriage."[6] And while this is true, it's not always correct. Sometimes friends evolve to fill in the gaps that are left by an inadequate or undesirable family life.

For me, this became clear and evident from when I was very little. My own family was anything but "normal." I loved my family, but I frequently felt out of place and wished I belonged to the family of a friend or attempted to marry into the family I babysat for at the age of 16. Not the best plan in hindsight.

My home life, while at times extremely happy and fulfilling, was also full of hardships. By the time I was four years old, I was already acting as a guide for my completely blind older and only sibling, Jodi. She was a badass. Despite her disability, she never let anything stop her. I learned early on that being differently abled was anything but a "dis." She obviously had some specialized needs, but she always retained her sense of self and humor. She would, at times, bump into a wall on purpose and exclaim, "Oops! I didn't see it!" And not for nothing, my maiden name was Look. "Look, Dana!" "Where?" Look, Jodi!" "I can't." Kids are so brutal.

---

6 "family, n.1.1." OED Online, Oxford University Press, July 2018, https://en.oxforddictionaries.com/definition/family. Accessed 1 November 2018.

I loved Jodi and enjoyed being needed by her. At the behest of my mother, I'd care for her and escort her to a friends' house down the block so that she'd be integrated with "regular" friendships. Bless my mom for that. She really did crusade on behalf of my sister and is very much the reason for my strong need for advocacy.

Despite all that, I frequently found myself wishing I were a part of a "normal" family. Where moms and dads get along. Where siblings love and fight and love again. Where meals are eaten together, and sometimes intense topics are discussed and debated. My mom's undiagnosed but clear bipolar disorder, obsessive-compulsive disorder, and hypochondria severely strained the relationships within the family. The highs were fun and some of my best memories of her. The lows meant run and hide. They're some of my worst memories of her. She was suffering, of course, but none of us really knew what to do about it or how to acknowledge it. It created rifts and cracks in the foundations of our family life and within myself.

But as having a family severely decreases the chances of being adopted, I found myself adopting other friends and families. Today, I still continue to include my intimate circle of friends and their extended families with my core family of my husband, two wonderful daughters, and three adorable rescue dogs. When I think of the Generations facet, I include all of them. They are my family through and through. You get to define your family.

A lifelong habit of "people-collection" both serves and starves me throughout my life.

Draw Your Line

All this is easy for me to say now. But it took me a long time to get to this point: years of building relationships, setting boundaries, and defining my personal definition of family. It wasn't always like this. When you settle in the Generations facet and allow yourself to be pressured or guilted into something that isn't your choice, it can put a real strain on the relationship, whether you realize it or not.

After I had my beautiful first daughter, Ava, I suffered from a serious bout of post-partum depression (I cover this in more detail in the "Life As a Business" Chapter). After my recovery, I was hesitant to have a second child. What if I relapsed? What if it was worse this time and I wouldn't recover? But my ex-husband had so much faith in me and I wanted to give Ava a sister, so we tried very hard to have our second child. Thankfully, I had no post-partum symptoms after Annika's birth. These two girls are my world and I'm grateful to this day that I made the right decision and didn't let fear stop me.

After Annika, however, I decided no more kids. I was happy with our two wonderful daughters. My ex-husband, however, kept insisting on having four kids. Not wanting to tempt fate and experience the hell I'd gone through before, I offered to adopt. He didn't want to, so we stopped at two kids. This would end up being the beginning of the end for our marriage, among many other messy details which are not relevant to this story or coming from a place of my highest self. Today, the relationship I have with my ex is better than it's ever been. I'm so grateful that he is and forever will be their dad.

When you look at this specific scenario, you can see that, although it ended up being the right decision, I settled. And I did. But the point is that I made the *conscious* choice to do so, after weighing the facts against my values. I settled smart. I knowingly made the compromise to have my second daughter. And when it came to my ex-husband asking for more, I drew a clear line in the sand and stood my ground. I was clear in what I wanted and how far I was willing to go. On that, I did not compromise because it was non-negotiable.

Compromise is not demise. When done consciously and honestly, it's how you Settle Smart and make the right choice *for you!*

Around this time, I was very fortunate to meet two incredible women and role models, both of whom would occupy the rest of my life and will forever hold a precious spot in my heart. I was working in a nonprofit, in what I called my "heart job," given my passion toward helping others and being more available and close to home while my daughters were little. Interestingly, I was the development director at Coast Side Family Medical Clinic in my hometown of Half Moon Bay, Northern California, fundraising while pregnant with my second daughter. In one of the most serendipitous moments of my life, I met Susie, a super-positive, glass-is-half-full, retired exec, now gourmet, artist, and donor on my fundraising committee, and Beverly, also a donor and a high-tech, kick-ass, women's-movement-type CEO. Susie became the mom I'd always wanted but never had. Beverly became my fairy godmother, who would end up ordained and marrying me, my second and final time. My maternal mother was still alive, but sadly, practically reclusive at that time and in Wisconsin.

Susie had quite a few "Susieisms." But the one that really resonated with me remains something that applies to all people, young and old alike: "You are your own best friend."

Practice Makes Permanent, Not Perfect

Yosemite

We have an annual tradition in our family, including Susie and my former nanny of ten years, jiujitsu black belt, athlete, adventurer, ass-kicker, and lifelong friend Charlene. Every year we go on a vacation to somewhere rich in nature. During these vacations, we try to find challenging hikes with wonderful vistas to explore. Unlike my family, I'm not a big hiker. I go on these trips to spend time with them and to enjoy nature. So, often the hikes that we find get so intense that I opt out and instead live vicariously through the stories and pictures my family brings back.

Two summers ago, we went to Yosemite and challenged ourselves to walk up the Vernal Falls trail. And we reached it! Fantastic! I was so exhausted, I just wanted to sit down and enjoy the waterfall from the shade of the trees. My family, being the overachievers that they are, wanted to keep going to the top of Nevada Falls. Despite the darkening daylight and every ounce of my body yelling at me to not go on, I gave into the choruses of "Come on!" and "You can do it!"

Now, if you've never hiked up to Nevada Falls via the Mist Trail, let me give you a word of caution. Don't do it. I mean, unless you're really sure. You hike up right next to the waterfall, which is lovely until you realize that the mist from the waterfall makes everything slippery. So now you can't enjoy the view because you're staring at your feet, arms thrown out to the side, in a desperate attempt to not slip on the slick, mossy steps. You gain a newfound appreciation for dry ground, let me tell you, so sturdy and unlikely to make you fall flat on your face. Really, dry ground is the unsung hero of everyday life.

Then, after the Slippery Trail of Death, you come upon ... dry ground! At last!

You breathe a sigh of relief until you look up and realize, oh no, an incline and then stairs. Not just any stairs. Stairs made for GIANTS. Seriously, the clearance on some of those steps came up to my waist. Okay, I'm exaggerating, but not as much as you'd think— I'm pretty short. So after spending fifteen precarious minutes trying to pick up your feet as little as possible in order not to slip, you now have to raise them to midcalf or knee height to climb these stone steps. As you huff and puff your way up a very steep incline, giving your legs a pep talk in an effort to convince them not to fail you now, a five-year-old sprints by you—laughing—completely destroying any sense of accomplishment you may have had up to this moment. Not to mention my sixteen-year-old was starting to struggle by the end, so in addition to my exhaustion, regret, and a growing feeling of resentment toward five-year-olds, I was now worried about my daughter. I was completely and utterly distressed.

But after my daughters got their second wind, what felt like an eternity of hardships, and my near-continuous contemplation of how much a rescue helicopter would cost me, we made it to the top of Nevada Falls.

The view was breathtaking. The clear waters cascaded down into a lush, evergreen forest. Mountains rose up all around, their dark blue and black hues silhouetted against a rose-colored sky. The air, clear and crisp, filled my lungs. I felt awe. I felt humility. And it was there, at the top of the waterfall that I'd fought to the top of, overlooking the raw beauty of the world, that I promised myself: never again.

That resolution cemented itself as I realized ... we had to hike back down. With the dark evening imminent and the last bus back to the parking area about to leave, we burst into a full sprint. I had no gas left in my tank, but with black-belt Charlene motivating me not to crumple into a heap, we somehow made it.

Contemplate this story for a moment. Do you think I settled here? Remember your answer as you read the next story.

Maui

This next year, my family and I went to Maui for our vacation. For our hike this time, I, by a random chance of last-minute trail scouring, found the Bamboo Forest. The description looked like exactly what we wanted with hikes that centered around waterfalls and streams. I also found some nice short hiking trails that looked easy enough for me and led to two or three waterfalls, as well as harder trails for the more able climbers in our group (read: everyone else). This was a perfect cliff-jumping area for the family and a serene writing area for me.

If you ever go to this forest, the first sight you see is the verdant bamboo forest. Enveloped in cool green air, we let the kids navigate the paths. As we hiked on and on and on … and on … we started to realize, we hadn't seen any people in a long while. Chalking it up to a strange coincidence, we plowed on, enjoying the slightly challenging but invigorating hike and eagerly awaiting the promised waterfall at the end.

But the trail wouldn't end. And the hike started getting more and more challenging.

Finally, we ran into a couple who looked much more adventurous than we did, and they kindly informed us that we were completely off-path. Charlene, the fearless leader of our group, volunteered to scout ahead to see if she could find a path. About fifteen minutes later, her voice rang through the bamboo that there was no path and we needed to double back.

So we started hiking down, which I realized as we turned around, meant hiking down a sheer cliff side. Clinging onto the bamboo for dear life, I slowly started back. The kids loved it, rushing past me, basically using the bamboo as a way to gain momentum. Finally, after bouts of cursing, yelling, and "woohoos!" we found a way down the cliff: scaling down the side using overhanging bamboo as rope.

Oh yeah, I was terrified. My eldest waited for me at the bottom, letting me know she would catch me. That didn't help.

Finally, even I made it down the cliff, and we rejoined civilization and hiked the rest of the way to the waterfall for lunch. Tired and shaken by this point, I became aware that my family was, once again, excited about something. I looked up to see them pointing at something ladder-esque and thought, "How does *that* qualify as a ladder?" Of course, after a quick rest, my family was invigorated and wanted to climb up the (k)not-ladder. It was Vernal Falls all over again. Only this time, I knew better. Ignoring the pleas, I wished my family good luck, settled down in a nice shady area with a view of the waterfall, and worked on my book. This book to be exact!

Now, contemplate this story. Did I settle here?

Did I Settle?

In the first story, I went against my better judgment. I gave in to the pressures of others instead of paying attention to what my body was telling me. That's settling. Although I made the choice consciously, I overrode my line in the sand because I felt like I *should* go to the top. So, even though I made it and it was an achievement, it pushed me over my line.

With the bamboo forest, given the added intensity that we didn't know about—namely trailblazing—I knew I'd reached the peak of my personal best for that day. So, had I pushed myself because everyone else wanted me to, I would've been settling. I would have taken away from my highest peak of the day by doing something that didn't actually serve me. I knew I was done. I did not need that second milestone, nor did I want it.

Communication Is Key

While this tip will resurface throughout the book, it's crucial here as your family are probably the people you interact with the most. In business the expectations of you are set clearly, usually through a contract or job description. Marriage and partnerships operate in a similar way. Right from the beginning, communicate clearly about where you are and are not willing to settle. What is important to you that you will not compromise? Communicate this to your partner and have them do the same. Listen with care and create and adapt to a life schedule that works for both of you. For example, in my marriage today, we don't always live together full-time. I look forward to my time with myself, my daughters, and my dogs. But I always really look forward to my husband coming back, as well. It works for us.

When my hubby Darren and I met four years ago, neither of us was looking, nor in a position to enter into a serious relationship. We were, however, totally aligned in terms of our values, beliefs, life desires, and connection with one another. When a partnership is truly that—a partnership—it is equal. Not equal like equality, but equal like give and take, yin and yang, a mirror to show one another the truth. When your relationship is equal, we've found that you're able to be yourself, truly and freely. There are no games, communication is very easy, and designing a life together that works for both of us as individuals as well as a team is simple! Trust me, sisters and brothers, I kissed a lot of frogs to get my prince.

(Sorry to any former frogs reading this book, this is not meant to hurt your feelings. One girl's frog is another girl's prince!)

Finally, to bring things back to Shanti's quote from the beginning of the book, she communicates to her family her expectations and the things she wants to do. She is clear about what she's willing to do and what she isn't. She'll attend her children's major games but not every practice. This clear and honest communication allows her to make choices without guilt or the feeling of "should." She prioritizes what is important to her and compromises in the areas that aren't as important. This is the beginning, and the key, to enacting the Stop Settling method, mindset, and movement into your life. This is how you make sure that you Settle Smart.

Takeaways Brought to You by Fact Versus Fiction:

Fiction #1: Blood is thicker than water.

Fact #1: You, and only you, get to define your family. Blood of the covenant may be thicker than the water of the womb.

Fiction #2: Boundaries are only important when coloring.

Fact #2: Know your boundaries and communicate them clearly to your family. Make no apologies for what is important to you. Your family loves you; they will value your honesty.

Fiction #3: Peer pressure is only for teens.

Fact #3: Peer pressure happens every time you feel guilty or you tell yourself you "should" be doing something. That's an outside influence trying to tell you your values.

Fiction #4: My kids love me less when I don't keep up with them.

Fact: #4: Your family will respect your honesty if you communicate your passions and guidelines honestly and kindly.

Fiction #5: Traditional value systems and approaches are the only ones that work.

Fact #5: Everybody is different, so everyone's family is different. Traditional value systems and approaches are just one of many ways to live your life.

Fiction #6: By making trade-offs and compromises, I am inferior.

Fact #6: As long as you make them *consciously*, trade-offs and compromises are how you indicate to your family, and to everyone else around you, what you hold valuable and worth your time.

4

CIRCLE

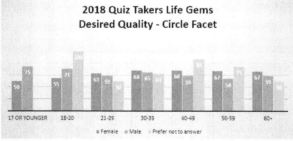

In the Circle facet, things appear steady across both ages and genders hovering around the Neutral and Infrequently Settling in the Current Life Gems while desiring to either stay or move up to Infrequently Settling. We also see some spikes into the Never Settling way of living in this facet.

What is Circle?

THE CIRCLE FACET is comprised of the enriching and exciting experiences that come from being around friends. A good group of friends is fun, accepting, and one of the best support networks you can have. True friendships are intimate, close, and tightknit.

Toxic Friendships

The Circle facet is realized in a true group of friends. What do I mean by a *true* group of friends? If someone is a true friend, your relationship with them is not codependent but equal. There is a healthy give and receive.

While true friendships can be the most uplifting and empowering part of your life, toxic friendships will bleed you dry. They will take away your energy and joy, and severely hinder your ability to be fulfilled in any other facet. They'll consume your daily life. Come on, you know the ones you have and have had.

If the relationship is codependent, that is red flag number one. If either you or the friend cannot function (and I really mean *function*) without each other, that's red flag number two. A couple of years ago, I took a long hard look at some of my friendships. What I realized was that my relationship with one of my close girlfriends, among some others, was completely and very detrimentally codependent. I felt compelled to always be there for them, to answer for my actions to them, to put them above and beyond everyone and everything else in my life. They were number one and so help me if I ever let them slip into the number-two spot.

With one particular relationship, it was the best of times, it was the worst of times. When we'd travel, we'd have the best time. I'd work and do my business-y thing. She'd go shopping and enjoy the amenities of whatever city we were visiting. The worst of times included things like a bitter and ugly separation between her and her husband that would never lead to divorce. And sadly, one son who would become the son I never had. The other son, with severe addiction issues, would at one point culminate my attempt at healing their relationship with straight talk by verbally attacking me in their driveway. We followed this immediately (and I mean *immediately*) by a girl's getaway weekend, where the incident was never mentioned.

I still remember all of the good times fondly. The good times were really great, and they still bring a smile to my face when I think about them. But no matter what close friends we were, the relationship was codependent and unhealthy. It had to stop, for both our sakes.

This type of friendship is not worth your time or energy. Don't keep those types of friends around just because you think you need to have a lot of friends. *It's not worth it.* Prioritize what's important and be relentless about keeping what's best for you. If you come from a place of joy, honesty, and good intent, then you'll keep the healthy relationships and do away with the rest.

Quality over Quantity

Scoring high in the Circle Facet does not mean you need to be overloading yourself with friends. The notion that the more friends you have, the more you "fulfill" the criteria for the Circle facet is wrong. First of all, this isn't a healthy way to measure within the Circle facet. The criteria involve a lot of numbers and math pulled from your quiz results. Even if you only have three or four close friends, as long as you prioritize them and make the conscious decision to spend lots of time with them, it's better than having a multitude of "friends" whom you don't really know.

There's a reason I'm trying to caution you against the quality of friends you keep. If you're not selective in your friends, you may easily end up in a toxic friendship. Just as in every other facet, you must Settle Smart here! Understand what you want from a friendship and make that a non-negotiable line.

The Three Circles of Friends

I say this in the most loving way, but not all friends are created equal. Depending on your mutual interests, hobbies, etc., you will have friends with whom you connect on a deeper level.

After my realization of what I wanted from my friendships, I began to look at my friends in concentric circles. I found that my friends really fell into three areas: BFF Circle, Inner Circle, and Acquaintances. Not the most creative names, I know, but they illustrate the relationships perfectly.

The BFF Circle is my smallest circle, only comprised of three people, my husband and my bicoastal best friends, Tam and Em. They are both simply the best. When I am with these people, I'm always my authentic self. We are all equals and our relationships are built on mutual respect, collaboration, honesty, and trust.

The next layer out, with one degree of separation from the BFF circle, is my Inner Circle. The circle here is wider and has more people. These are the handful of people who really know me and vice versa. Our main areas of passion and interest align, and I know we have each other's backs.

From that circle out is the Acquaintance Circle—the largest circle. I know that the word often makes it seem like these are people who are distant from me for some negative reason, but that's not the case. These are people whom I like but our interests and passions aren't aligned. The number here is limitless. What matters here is how much time I want to spend with them and how much depth is there.

Now you may disagree with me here, but for the most part, I don't actively try to raise people from the Acquaintance Circle into the Inner Circle, and so on. I used to be the type of person who would dedicate inordinate amounts of time to that. Not anymore.

Think about businesses and their "friends"—their partners. Most businesses tier their partners into different groups and channels, from comarketing, to reselling, to strategic alliances, and even the most intimate, joint ventures. Strategic alliances and joint ventures are notoriously hard to make work and consist of very short lists of possible partners who fit together like a zipper or a hand and glove.

If you've experienced the ups and downs of mergers and acquisitions in the business world, many times the difficulty in integrating the two companies into one comes from the cultural differences that lie beneath the surface and when stressed blows up even before the deal is closed, or along the way when the ink has dried and now you are faced with bringing divergent people together. This is partly why mergers and acquisitions are so hard to integrate, even if you do consummate that type of marriage, which tends to blow up along the path to buying and selling. I've lived through that in business more times than I can count, on both sides of the equation.

It's like that in personal relationships too. Those that are highly integrated and intertwined yield a high return for both parties. The general partnership types, or the lowest level, have a lot more partners. But the relationships are more distant, the amount of work put into the relationship is minimal, and the return is also small. This is that same concept.

The reality is that there is only so much of me to go around and only so much time I want to spend in this facet. So I want to spend my time where it's most valuable for myself and the other person involved. I guess, in the end, I've become a bit like my father in this regard.

Takeaways Brought to You by Fact Versus Fiction:

Fiction #1.1: Just like in high school, we have tons of BFFs.

Fiction #1.2: By being highly selective of whom I'm close to and spend time with, I am a bad person and friend.

Fiction #1.3: One size fits all. We are human and therefore MUST be social.

Fact #1: Consciously deciding what types of people you choose to surround yourself with fulfills and helps you grow as a person, while overloading yourself with too many people who aren't aligned with you will drain you.

Fiction #2: All introverts are antisocial. All extroverts want to be around people all the time.

Fact #2: Introverts may be social. Extroverts may need time away from other people.

Fiction #3: I should keep a friend around even if the relationship is toxic because I don't want to hurt their feelings.

Fact #3: By ending toxic friendships, you will create more space for those with whom you actually want to spend time.

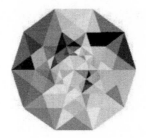

SOCIETY

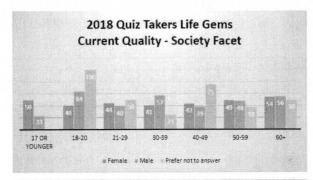

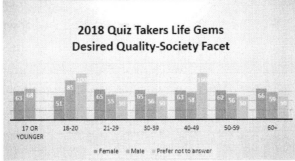

Unfortunately, this facet does not seem to resonate as much with our quiz-takers as scoring hovers around Infrequently Settling and Neutral with a little uplift towards Infrequently Settling. This feels like a microcosm of our world issues. If we all did more for our communities and society at large, what impact would we make? Public service announcement over.

THE SOCIETY FACET is all about belonging. It's dominated by selfless participation that furthers our connection with our community, neighborhood, schools, and/or faith.

THE WAY WE give back to our community is very individualized. It may be as simple as writing a check to an organization or nonprofit or as complex as organizing a community garden.

Once a year during the holidays, my family and I try to give back somehow. One of the most touching and gratifying acts we did was going down to a barrio to give gifts to the less fortunate children. One time, while we were there, a baby was playing in a pile of rocks in the backyard of a house. The mother saw us and lifted her child over the fence. In a touching moment, Annika gave her the necklace that I had given her many years ago. I was so proud of her. That brief moment instilled values and humility in all of us for years to come. And I was able to hold that precious little girl, which was the gift to me.

For me, this is the area where I still feel I am settling habitually rather than consciously. I want to be more proactive and spend more time in this facet, as advocacy has always been such a large part of my life. However, I keep finding excuses or reasons as to why I simply don't have enough time. I'm sharing this with you so that you know that the journey to Settling Smart doesn't happen overnight. It will take time, dedication, and patience with yourself!

What is Society?

My definition of Society and giving back has evolved over the years.

As I've shared, when I was young, my feelings around society and giving back were fairly centered around my family and the disability community. Other causes or even my own community didn't seem as important to me. As I grew older, my view of the world widened to include my community and others trying to do good. I wanted to be a part of my community.

But I've always felt frustration around giving back. I always want to do and give more while knowing that both time and money have limits. These limits are unique to each of us as human beings.

Note: To superwomen and men everywhere. You *do* have a limit. You are human. Robots need not apply.

Do you ever feel that you want to do more in society? That even though you may do as much as you are able to, it still gnaws at you?

For me, it's almost like a constant hum in the back of my mind. And the volume on that hum turns way up when I see or experience something in society that feels wrong to me. For example, when I'm driving to our local Starbucks, pet store, and supermarket, all within a small shopping center in our small coastal town, there tend to be homeless people on the same corner where you turn in and out of the shopping center. My daughters and I have given them food, a little money, even pet supplies when these folks have dogs with them. But it still breaks my heart. I wonder, how do we solve for this massive and growing homeless and hunger situation? It's happening in our own communities, literally, in our own backyards. My family and I try to contribute to international organizations to help out those in impoverished countries, and while that feels good, I always have this gnawing feeling that I want to be doing more for our local community instead of focusing my efforts elsewhere. I wish I were Mother Teresa, but I'm not.

I often ponder, what are we able to do that's sustainable? How do we start to solve for the world's most staggering issues?

The answer for me lies in the power that comes from giving itself. No matter how large or small the gift of time, cash, food, or any other type of giving that we do, by giving alone, we are doing enough. If each and every one of us shifts our mindset to one of giving and takes some form of action toward it, things will change for the better. Every little bit counts. This is my new definition of charity that starts at home. Perhaps you will join me in giving just a bit more. Whatever you are willing and *able* to give, it counts. It has to! And, it's enough.

The Giving Tree

As I've mentioned, advocacy and fighting for the underdog, was and is my jam. The list of causes, passion projects, and socially conscious ventures that I either endorse or try to participate in is as eclectic and multidimensional as I am. Take a moment and list your own ways of giving, what's working for you and not? Where might you settle a little less when it comes to giving back. If we gave more, created a ground swell, the world would simply be a happier, healthier, more equitable place. It's not a coincidence that most of the early quiz takers considered themselves settling more than they would like in the area of Society and Activism.

Here's my list, and even though it's long and multidimensional, it still doesn't feel like I give as much as I want to and as a family, as much as we aspire to...

Fundraisers

Worked as a fundraiser/fortune teller at our home-based annual summer carnival for the Lion's Club camp for my sister and other special needs kids.

Countless angel tree and adopt-a-family programs in our local, coastal community.

Volunteering

Official Hugger at the Special Olympics.

Swim-program volunteer with my daughter who was two at the time, for kids with cerebral palsy and other developmental issues.

Countless volunteer hours in our local theater, both before my youngest daughter got involved and during. My favorite was hair and make-up! One show had seventy-eight kids and eight performances … go Lion King! Added bonus: I was coaching an incredible MAC Cosmetics executive during these shows, and he was able to help this nonprofit local theater in our small town with serious discounts on the stage make-up that we would have had to fundraise three times as hard and long to be able to afford.

Remember, you don't get if you don't ask. People are so willing to help however they're able, and every little bit counts. This blew my mind from my nonprofit/fundraising days: Did you know that the average annual household income of families who give is sixty thousand dollars? That's *household*, people, not head of household only. The major donors are great and benevolent; however, there aren't enough to go around. It's the families closest to the poverty or working-poverty line that tend to give the most. Now stop and think about that for a minute, with everything you're learning from the Stop Settling mindset. What mindset do these families have when it comes to prioritizing their society facet? You got it: it's either at Infrequently Settling or Never Settling. Now, just to ensure you're with me and starting to apply the learning, what may need to occur sometimes when there are financial constraints or added needs in their own family? This happens to me all the time, especially having been a single mother for ten years. This is where that great adage "charity starts at home" kicks in. Then, we need to shift the dynamic a bit in the society facet in this example toward neutral or even frequently settling in order to make room (and resources, time, and money) for the Generations facet. These are great examples of clear, conscious, and unapologetic trade-offs.

Boards

Board of Directors, fundraiser, grant writer, whatever they needed, United Cerebral Palsy (UCP) in Milwaukee, Wisconsin.

Development Officer/Chief Business Officer, UCP Golden Gate (after transferring for work to California from Wisconsin, I transferred my board seat and then joined them as an employee, my entrée into the nonprofit world—my "heart job."

Development Director, Coastside Medical Clinic, Half Moon Bay (again, first as a volunteer, donor, and patient then joined as an employee). Launched a Just for Teens Clinic in our local community, before the Affordable Care Act, to help under- and uninsured families and teens receive treatment holistically.

Public-speaking training for young adults in nonprofits and my oldest daughter's high school, which was a charter/start-up at the time, all based in design thinking.

Reboot Accel, helping to get women current, connected, and confident to return to work with impact and influence

Donations

Localized giving in two different barrios while on vacation with small children. The first time was in Puerto Vallarta where the family we visited had many small children who had no idea what gum or coloring books and colors were. Together we all ate their amazing food and played with whatever stuff we had on us, plus the bubbles they blew with their *chicle*! The second time was where we try to vacation each year, in Playa del Carmen on the Yucatan Peninsula. My girlfriend lives there and took us into a barrio that was the juxtaposition of where my daughters and I were staying with some friends, and we went on a shopping spree at Walmart. It's incredible what one thousand dollars in gifts and toys will do for one's spirit when on the giving, not receiving end. I watched my then seven-year-old younger daughter, literally take the necklace off her neck and put it around the neck of a two- or three-year-old girl in her mother's arms. She was dirty and scared at first, but so clearly loved. The mother asked us to feed her a bottle and hold her; it was heaven. The gratefulness and hope in that young mom's eyes will be with me and my family forever.

Clothes drives, donations, and dress-for-success career support for women's shelters in the Bay Area.

Second Harvest during Thanksgiving, along with team-building at my last company, a tradition started by the founder and carried on by the next wave of leaders, myself included. Such a cool way to integrate teamwork and giving!

Organizations

Through the amazing nonprofit organization Kiva International, for six years I've been giving my leadership colleagues and customers the ability to fund small businesses around the world. I make the donation, acting as the funder, and everyone else gets to "shop" for a small-business owner whose work and story touches their heart.

The really cool thing is that the loan is paid back; then, you're able to reinvest that money again toward another small business. This type of sustainability really inspires me and thousands of individuals and corporations each year to give in this economically integrated way. Rosie from Sugarfina, who I featured in a CEO perspective callout in this book, uses Kiva in the same way. Go, Rosie!

My daughters and I selected and purchased a water buffalo one year from Heifer International during the holidays for one family in a developing country.

Takeaways Brought to You by Fact Versus Fiction:

Fiction #1.1: Writing a check for nonprofits is not a good enough way for someone to give back.

Fiction #1.2: Volunteering two times a year in your kid's school is the minimum to give back and feel good about your contribution.

Fiction #1.3: Reprioritizing your life to do more for your community makes you someone who is weak, not career-focused, or even potentially lazy when it comes to career.

Fiction #1.4: If you don't give back, you won't belong.

Fiction #1.5: Good is not good enough.

Fiction #1.6: Good is the enemy of great.

Fact #1: Your personal best is good enough, and most likely, not perfect. Perfect, like normal, is overrated. The majority of individual choices about how you give back, contribute, and participate, are as personal as our fingerprint. There is no right or wrong, good or bad. As long as you are genuine to your own goals, your own desires, and your own willingness to contribute, it's just right. Just do you. Remember charity starts at home. Sometimes that's for ourselves, for our community, or for our world. Do not judge yourself or others on how, when, and where they contribute.

6

VITALITY

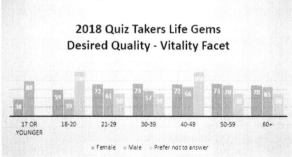

Here, we see people really taking the power of choice in hand (and body) as they make actionable decisions towards pulling back on extremes as well as incrementally shifting up toward more health, fitness, mental and spiritual wellness, etc. It also appears that women, overall, want to jump from Frequently Settling to Infrequently Settling, across most ages measured. Men, also have aspirations to be healthier, however, with slightly less vigor.

THE VITALITY FACET is about your health. This includes your physical, mental, and emotional wellness. And for those of you that roll this way, spiritual. It's all about uplifting yourself by living an active and centered lifestyle. The vitality facet takes into account not only your workout schedule but also your hobbies and how you deal with stress.

Work It!

Let's tackle the most obvious part of this facet first: working out. It's what most of us think of and try to improve on when we think about our health. The issue here is that most of us go from zero to one hundred too quickly and it ends up hindering our progress.

Take me, for example. I love working out, but I bore easily doing the same workouts over and over. If I found a workout I loved, I would push myself to complete it even if it meant injuring myself.

This is not healthy. This is not Settling Smart. Trying to improve your health but not caring if you get hurt is counterproductive.

A few years ago, I really got into Zumba. It was fast-paced and different every time—my kind of exercise. But after a few classes, I began to feel old injuries creeping up. If I'd been settling then, I would have just kept going. Instead, I first tried to modify the class to fit my abilities. When that didn't work, I had to give it up. I found other workouts, like Pilates, that aren't as strenuous on my body. By consciously making the choice to quit Zumba and finding other ways to work out, I'm no longer settling.

When it comes to physical exercise, make sure you're making incremental changes. If you're currently not working out but you want to get back into shape, set S.M.A.R.T. goals. For those of you in the business world, that acronym will be familiar. S.M.A.R.T. stands for Specific, Measurable, Achievable, Realistic, and Time-boxed. When setting your workout goals, make sure they meet those criteria. This will help you achieve your goals and build up your confidence. If you go from never working out to working out for two hours five days a week, you're going to have a very hard time and most likely will fail. Don't set yourself up for failure.

Don't row five days per week after you buy your sophisticated rowing machine. Build momentum and consistency. Start with three and see how you do.

And, for those of you who are new moms, here's a little tip: do not jump into Chaturanga yoga pose eight weeks after having a baby when your ligaments are still wonky. After my second daughter was born, I thought that having done yoga throughout my pregnancy, I would just continue. Well, power yoga at that time for my body was a very bad idea. That, coupled with me showing my yoga master that something was off in my right wrist, to which he replied that it happens a lot in yoga and I needed to "relax, relax"—and snap—he put my wrist back into place. Except that he didn't. I'd torn my dorsal ligament and I ended up in surgery, then was casted with a barbaric pin sticking out of my wrist. Trying to hold, feed, or do anything with my daughter without bonking her on the head with my cast was a serious, multiple-person effort.

Your Mind and You

As I mentioned earlier, this facet is about your well-being as much as it is about your physical health. We all have a lot to do. And, at times, it may feel like the pile just keeps growing and growing. That's why it's so important to make time for passion projects, hobbies, and just relaxation. By giving yourself and your brain a break, it helps recharge your battery. Focusing on your favorite hobby after a grueling day at work can give you the distance you need to unwind. If you're extroverted, take time to connect with people who inspire and motivate you. Go out with friends or family. Go see a movie or go out on the town. If you're more introverted, give yourself a break. Curl up with a good book or movie and just decompress from the pressures of the day.

What Do You Need?

This facet will shift up and down on the scale more than the other facets because it's so situational. If you had a long weekend in Vegas, you might find yourself craving a healthier lifestyle with fewer social interactions for a few days after. Or maybe you pulled a hamstring while hiking and need to rest it for the week. Listen to your body and your mind. Determine what you need based on that. Taking this break is vital to enhancing your performance.

I love that Arianna Huffington reminds us that our phones get recharged, one time per day, sometimes for a full twenty-four hours. We take better care of our electronics than ourselves.[7]

I want to point out a story about my own father here. He was kind of a loner but very happy and successful in his dental practice. When he was at work he was animated, interactive, and seemingly extroverted. But when he'd come home, he was an introvert. He was quiet, pensive, and wanted to spend his evenings in peace and quiet. Today we would call him an ambivert. Socially extroverted and personally introverted.

And the older he got, the more he leaned toward the introverted side of his personality.

---

7 Huffington, Arianna. The Sleep Revolution. Harmony, 2017.

He didn't want to visit his friends very often. He'd much rather solve *New York Times* crossword puzzles and send clues to his friends via email. Everything was about the cerebral and the intellectual.

I was convinced he was in the wrong.

This wasn't my idea of healthy relationships. This wasn't how I thought he should unwind from work. He should be out there, with people, enjoying activities. I was "shoulding" him to death. I tried so hard to get him to go out more and be less reclusive. I was convinced I knew best. I was worried he'd be lonely.

I was so wrong.

Whenever I thought about my father, it was always in the context of "I." *I wouldn't do this, so he's not doing it right.* My thoughts and rationalizations filled with "I would do this," and "I don't like that." I put my own ideals and how I wanted to be treated on him. It was all about me when it needed to be all about him.

Being reclusive made him happy in his later years. He'd already done the social scene for as long as he wanted to and experienced as much of it as he wished. As he became more quiet and subdued, he became more determined to operate within his own authenticity. Instead of spending hours with people he kind of liked, he spent much of his time with his daughter and grandchildren, the people that meant the world to him. He wasn't unhappy. He wasn't depressed. A little socially anxious, maybe, but he was his own authentically happy self. By increasing the value of the people he spent time with, he made the time he spent with people quality time. He played solitaire online. He taught other senior citizens to work a computer. He generated his own weekly quiz which was like "Jeopardy" on steroids. And he did his *New York Times* crossword puzzles while eating a pint of ice cream a day, sometimes as his dinner. That was his daily design for his 60 percent.

The way he lived his life was the model I had in mind when I was developing this quiz: a person beholden to no one's expectations of happiness but his/her own. If he were alive today, and I wish he were, his Life Gem would be Neutral in almost every facet other than Vitality. The Vitality facet would be firmly in Never Settling.

My father's definition of vitality was quite different from anyone else's. His definition was spending quality time with his family, crossword puzzles, his solitaire games, reading voraciously, watching his TV shows, eating ice cream, and, when the mood struck him, "kibitzing" with the neighbors.

If that was good enough for him, why wasn't it good enough for me?

Now that he's passed and I'm reflecting on dots to connect, it's clear that he did have some social anxiety. But that did not justify my selfish "help."

The Platinum Rule

I have my own answer to the Golden Rule. By treating others the way *we* would want to be treated, we take them out of the equation. It becomes all about us and our preferences over theirs. Which is ludicrous. The whole point of the Golden Rule is to foster understanding and harmony between people. How are you going to do that if you only consider yourself?

So, I've tweaked it a little and come up with my own Platinum Rule.

The Golden Rule: Do unto others as you would have them do unto you.

The Platinum Rule: Do unto others as they would have you do unto them.

By putting the other person back into the equation, you take them into account: their likes, dislikes, wants, and needs. It forces you to put yourself in someone else's shoes and act in a way that is beneficial and empathetic to them, not you.

Takeaways Brought to You by Fact Versus Fiction:

Fiction #1: If I start working out five days a week and I hit it, I will feel better about myself and get in shape faster.

Fact #1: People who hit incremental goals are able to increase successfully over time. The key to working out is frequency, duration, and being realistic, just like a S.M.A.R.T. goal in business. You have to be S.M.A.R.T. for your fitness goals, too.

Fiction #1: I know what's best for you and you're not my child. You're my dad, BFF, coworker, or employee.

Fact #2: Get inside people's heads and hearts, then go for platinum. It's more valuable than gold.

THE MINDSET

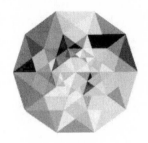

7

The Business of Life is NOT Life As a Business

LIFE WRAPS AROUND all the different facets. You cannot separate work from your life and you cannot separate life from your work. It's all about Settling Smart and making conscious choices about where you make compromises and trade-offs. The choices you make intertwine with the whole of your life and touch every facet in one way or another. So what happens at work affects the various facets of your life and vice versa. It's not enough to be a leader only at work. Be a leader throughout your life. It's all connected. Your abilities as a leader at work directly support how you are at home and vice versa.

Let's take a peek into the generic morning of a working professional (namely me, circa 2010). If I'd had the Stop Settling quiz back then, my Gem would have been charcoal black. I was a Never Settler. I believed I could do everything without having to compromise or make trade-offs. I was a supermom, a superboss, a damn superhero.

The alarm goes off.

You shake yourself awake and convince yourself that it's a good idea to get out of bed. You get ready, grab coffee and a bite to eat, usher (or wrangle) the kids into the car, and take them to school. You drop them off and begin the traffic-ridden journey to work.

As you sit in the slow trudge, you start to think about everything you're going to do at work. The more you think about it, the more you transform.

Your supposedly weaker qualities fade into the background while strong power words like focused, motivated, organized, and dedicated rise up. Sitting in your car, you mold yourself until you embody the qualities of a "true leader." You exit your car with more purpose and confidence than when you entered.

The day passes. The clock ticks by. You send off that last email and pack up to head out. It's the end of the workday. You say goodbye to whomever you see on the way down and head to your car. Small jokes are exchanged about the amount of hours in the day (or lack thereof) as well as laments about doing it all again tomorrow.

You get back into your transformation-mobile and drive to your next destination.

Regardless of where this is—picking up kids, home, gym, groceries, etc.—you transform again. The strong power words dissolve and are replaced by the humbler traits of being caring, attentive, funny, relaxed. You shed your suit and put on your comfy pants.

This false metamorphosis is incorrectly assumed to make you a better leader. I know I certainly thought it did. But the cycle of changing from caterpillar to butterfly back to caterpillar is exhausting and stagnating. You never move forward. You just flit back and forth between incomplete versions of yourself. I was convinced that I had to be one way in the office and another around my family and friends.

When I was working, I was running a company. I was kicking ass at my job. I was *leading* my career. When I wasn't, I was enjoying life. I was playing with my kids. I was grabbing a drink with friends. I was taking my dogs for a walk. The two worlds had nothing to do with each other. Each day, I left my "life" behind when I went to work and became my "work self." Then, when I left work, I left my "work self" behind and reconnected with my "life." I thought I could do everything without having to choose or make trade-offs.

I was wrong. And my mistaken beliefs became hazardous to my health.

I crashed in 2000. *Hard.* No, I'm not talking about a Silicon Valley tech-bubble bust in my own backyard. I'm talking about my own bust.

I hope the deep personal experience and sequencing I'm about to unpack helps you. It's hard to share, yet so important to the Stop Settling Mindset and Movement. I'm convinced it has reached its time to launch. Fair warning: I'm going to detail out how my self-denial and drive to "do it all by being my all" led to my suicide attempt. If this is triggering for you, feel free to skip to the next section.

Here's my story.

After the birth of my beautiful, sweet, and curious first daughter, Ava, I suffered from some serious postpartum issues— and consequently dealt with it like all good type-A, overachieving, superwoman, work-life balancing heroines do. I gave myself the internal daily pep rally, "You can have it all by doing it all. Now put on your big-girl panties and get on with it!" I never truly dealt with the issue, just assuming "this too shall pass."

I never took the time to acknowledge the depth of my state of mind. So when my boss asked me to return at eight weeks instead of three months to teach a global class of executives how to sell and play nicer together in the proverbial sandbox, I heard my voice say, "Okay." Never mind that I thought the request was ridiculous and outrageous. I was strongly encouraged to come back early, and I couldn't imagine a different response to the one I gave. I was so sure that my "baby blues" would pass.

My soon to be rebel thyroid and barely functioning pituitary gland had different ideas.

I pushed forward. Everything began falling into place: a new job with a team I loved and a beautiful bouncing baby girl. But like with all bullet wounds covered with Band-Aids, my symptoms started leaking out.

No matter.

I'm fine.

I was freezing, barely eating, barely sleeping, and starting to feel downright sick.

Okay. Maybe I'll go see a doctor.

Enter, family physician and OBGYN working together. They added more meds to my growing regiment. A mild antidepressant, never mind that hadn't had a mood swing in my life, let alone depression. But it let me sleep so I felt a little better.

That's good enough. Don't need to do anything more, just soldier on.

The time came for a med change. Since I didn't want to feel so numb, they thought, why not try a new designer drug? In this critical-thinking approach, I'd get off two pills and go down to one that would "do it all."

The irony didn't escape me.

Now, with groggy sleep, a full work schedule, baby care before and after work, no appetite, a major irritable bowel, and zero energy, I went back to my local family physician. He ran a battery of tests, looking for the cause for this terrible digestive disorder. He concluded that it must be bacterial and a coincidence. It wasn't.

I felt doomed. I had nowhere to go.

My life was like watching a movie. I became disconnected from everything around me. I saw myself mastermind a plan out of this life. My own ability to think critically and logically became totally skewed by medication I was having a horrible and adverse reaction to, which went unnoticed by everyone, including my doctors. Thinking of my lifelong dreams to watch my child grow up, let alone all the other responsibilities that I had signed up for in my first-in-line style, I knew what I had to do.

I took my sleeping pills and new designer drug, crushed up as many as I could, put them into something that seemed appetizing, and mixed it all together. I wrote a note to my husband, father, and daughter, and stuck it inside the Bible I'd bought in a final, desperate attempt to find salvation despite having been brought up as a non-practicing Jew. I put it on my pillow and told the entire lot of them I was going for a beach walk across our very heavily trafficked Highway 1. I crossed the street, went down to my favorite bench, and ate my concoction. The rest passed in a blur.

Amid the fog of my drugged-out mind, I somehow managed a moment of clarity. I headed back home but I was starting to falter. I have no idea how I crossed that highway or how I made it into my house. My father, husband, and baby girl noticed my strange and sad behavior, so unlike my usually peppy, go-get-'em, high-energy, love-the-world personality. I recall my father took one look at me and asking what I'd taken. And then I crashed. Right on my living room carpet. My dad, husband, and the local small-town EMTs saved my life.

After a short sabbatical from work, one week in the "ward," a psychiatrist who cared deeply and listened, my relentless research, and my endocrinologist, I was back on the right track. We finally concluded that a combination of my (previously unknown to me) family history, bad reactions to medicine, and determination to Never Settle had caused my downward spiral.

I've never written all this down, although I've told the story in helping others going through similar challenges. It doesn't seem like my own life I'm writing about here. It's all so strange to put all this in the middle of a business-meets-self-help book in order to launch this Method, Mindset, and Movement. However, I want to share it. I wouldn't be where I am today without this pivotal and unbelievably painful period in my life. Perhaps I wouldn't have this unwavering yearning to help others, even one person, to wake up and realize that their life is a precious Gem. We are all diamonds, some rougher than others, but so what? We all count.

The lesson learned here is that getting help, medical or otherwise, is not settling! If you need the meds, take them! I don't care what anyone tells you or what their own horror story was. However, take them with your eyes wide open. Be your own medical advocate and R&D department. Know your family history and constantly be aware. If you feel off, you are off. Please, ladies and gentlemen, do not shove it down or push through it as if you'll earn some badge of honor. My story is not unique. Look at the number of tragic endings that have occurred while I've been writing this book in mid-2018. We've lost Kate Spade, Anthony Bourdain, Avicii, Chris Cornell, and Chester Bennington to suicide within the past year, just to name a few. A study led by the University of Bergen examined 16,426 working adults and found an association between workaholism and psychiatric problems.[8] If you are experiencing mental health issues and you don't have help from loved ones, for whatever reason, please reach out!

The separation of my work and my "life," switching between the two, and my desired to Never Settle in any aspect drove me to insanity. The way I showed up in 20 percent of my life nearly took 100 percent of it.

I thank you for hanging in there with me to learn about this, why I shared it, and how it may help you or someone you know—if not today, then tomorrow.

Onto Lighter Things

You're fooling yourself if you think you can separate the different facets of your life. They all intertwine and interact with each other. Making choices about what matters to you and adjusting your priorities accordingly is how you become the person you want to be.

My story is extreme but real, and more common than society allows us to believe. But it's true for smaller events as well. Stress at work translates to irritability at home. Burnout from work causes burnout through every facet.

Thankfully, this holds true for positive things as well. Having dinner with your family every night or going hiking on the weekends gives you time to unwind and focus on things you love. This, in turn, boosts your spirits, which puts you in better health. If you're happy, you perform better at work. It's as simple as that. The triumphs and positive attributes you exhibit at work follow you into your other

---

8 Ratner, Paul. "Workaholics Have Serious Psychiatric Disorders, Researchers Find." Big Think, Big Think, 5 Oct. 2018, bigthink.com/paul-ratner/workaholics-have-a-surprising-amount-of-psychiatric-disorders.

facets. And the positive attributes in your "personal life" improve your work.

By decoupling these two facets of ourselves and treating the worlds as different, we detract from our ability to be happy, holistic, and effective in our careers, family, community, and so on. There is a business about life, but you don't treat life as a business. I'm guilty of that myself. Look for the balance sheet (contributions, purpose, and quality), not the balance scorecard where you lose the blend of art and science.

Being the Leader of Your Life

So what is a leader? The *Oxford English Dictionary* defines a leader as "The person who leads or commands a group, organization, or country."[9] But there's so much more to it than that. A true leader inspires those around them and pushes them to be better. They lead by example both at work and outside of it. People follow a true leader of their own accord. They don't need to be told to follow them.

Being a leader in your life is not just about being a CEO or a leader at work. It's about taking that same principle of being a great leader for yourself and others and applying it to both your office and out-of-office life. This includes things like leading by example and not asking others to do things you haven't done or wouldn't do.

If you want employees to feel like you, as an executive, leader, manager, etc., care about them, don't just preach company values at them. Walk through the office or your department in the morning and talk to people. Wish them a good morning, ask them how their day/week/weekend was, and really listen to their response. And

---

9 "leader, n.1." OED Online, Oxford University Press, July 2018, https://en.oxforddictionaries.com/definition/leader. Accessed 1 November 2018.

contribute to the conversation. Let them know what you did over the weekend. Create a dialogue.

It seems strange that I'm coaching you on how to have a conversation, but often times, especially at work, the "management" seems to forget that the people who work for them are human. This may not be the case. But if you never show it, how will they know?

Now, before you get ahead of yourself, I don't mean you ever treat your friends and family as your employees. Don't mentally fire your teenager just because she refuses to do her share of the household chores. Don't mentally put your friend on a performance plan because he showed up late to your dinner plans. However, do bring the positive aspects of being a leader that people want to follow to all aspects of your life. Do showcase your passion and dedication to your family. Do inspire and encourage your friends to take the risks that make them nervous. Do rally your local volunteer group to meet their goals for the food drive. Take the leader that embodies all those power words—the leader people want to follow—and put him/her in some comfy pants.

I always had these business plans to start my own company sitting on a shelf. I had a running list of people who I felt were both rockstars and superstars that I wanted to round out my own strengths in a dream-team concept for my company, mission-based, socially conscious, and absolutely filled with positive commerce. The triple threat. What I've realized is that I am coaching my dream team and creating a universal dream team through my work with others. I'm giving back, coaching, and learning from my clients. It's all one giant petri dish to create a universal team that will change the world.

The Leader People Want to Follow

I consider myself a corporate defector. It's not that I'm anticorporate, it's just that I'm prohuman and corporations aren't people. People join companies and leave companies the majority of the time for three common reasons: leadership, culture, and opportunity for growth and development. By being a great leader (and working for the corporation that's the right fit for you), you can solve two of the three issues. Lead well and pay attention to those you lead, and you can provide them opportunities for growth and development.

I think one of my biggest gripes with this decoupling behavior that tends to stem from the work-life balance myth, is that it leaves something important behind: ourselves. All those characteristics and quirks that make us unique, interesting, and fallible. Human. We don't need to mold ourselves into the ideal leader. The ideal leader is unattainable and unsustainable. No matter how high you rise, you are human, with likes and dislikes, faults and strengths. So, bring those less audacious adjectives with you to work. Be humorous, caring, relaxed, whatever! Coupled with good leadership skills and those strong power words, they will elevate you from a good leader to a great one who people want to follow.

An incredible example of this is Mark Sebba, former CEO of Net-a-Porter. If you haven't seen his fantastic send-off from Net-a-Porter, check it out on YouTube! The whole company threw him a flash-mob send-off to thank him for his time at the company. Now, here is a man who understands the importance of bringing humanity to the business culture! Blending the two promotes a better work environment with happier, more productive workers. Mark was kind enough to sit down with me and discuss his philosophy on building a supportive business culture.

Perhaps one of the most profound methods he brought to me was on the mix of talent. He credits a book called *Inside Her Pretty Little Head* as the inspiration for this method.

> Their premise was that men tended to be systematizers—and the "tended" is very important—and the women tended to be empathizers. Obviously, you could find plenty of examples of men who are empathizers and women who are systematizers and lots of people who merge in between, but those were the tendencies. We then, at the same time as the executive group, did the Myers-Briggs Testing and it told us a lot about us that we already knew, but it was actually quite an interesting exercise that we all went through. We expanded it to the rest of the managers in the company in a slightly different way, but again it was personality exercises to understand the sort of person you were and to understand the sort of person your colleague was. So, what we tried to do with it in the business was to partner people with complementary skills so that somebody who was very analytical would be paired with someone who was much softer and fuzzier. And in the buying, somebody with an "I" would be paired with someone very numerate. It all sounds hugely common-sensical, and it is, but that is what we tried to do and we were relatively successful at that.[10]

"Relatively" is Mark's way of saying *hugely*. The company is famed for its mix of talent, and the application of the opposite complements not only helped them become successful but stay a successful and pleasant place to work.

---

10 Sebba, Mark. Personal interview. 18 Jan. 2018.

Of course, creating a cohesive, pleasant environment that values people while holding them to higher expectations is not achievable without a lot of hard work and determination from the higher-ups. It all starts at the top.

Net-a-Porter solved for this by creating BLESS, the invention of cofounder Natalie Massenet and their head of human resources. BLESS stands for Be the best, Lead don't follow, Exceed expectations, Smart and stylish, and Start with yourself. But the principle, while extremely successful at Net-a-Porter as an award system and way for managers to appraise and incentivize people without sacrificing the cohesive culture, is applicable outside the workplace.

> It's all about leading by example. When I left, people wrote little notes for me, and one of the things that a lot of people said was that "I really liked how he walked through the office every morning and said, 'Good Morning' to me." It was only after I left that I realized why it matters to people. But to me it was the most obvious thing in the world.[11]

Successful leaders are more than just people who are in a position above others in the corporate hierarchy. They understand the importance of culture, fit, and the people who work for them. At the root of it all, a truly great leader cares. Both in the business and outside of it.

---

11 Sebba, Mark. Personal interview. 18 Jan. 2018.

When Life As a Business is Settling Versus Settling Smart

Settling Smart	Unconscious Settling
Have a plan and work your plan. In business, we plan. Oh, there are goals upon goals. And for each goal, there is a plan to execute against. Use this meticulousness when devising plans for other parts of your life. Want to build a garden in your backyard? Stick it in a project plan with dates and dependencies. Want to save for that vacation to Hawai'i with your family? Pull a budget together. Set S.M.A.R.T. (Specific, Measurable, Achievable, Realistic, and Time-boxed) goals for your dreams.	*Top down communication with a life partner doesn't work.* Telling your partner what/how/ when they should be doing things and skipping the why is a recipe for an unfulfilling relationship and guaranteed to lead to nasty fights.
Little to no blindsiding Communication is key in an office. You don't work in a vacuum. You're constantly communicating with your team and superiors about the status of various projects and tasks. Apply that clear communication to the other facets of your life. Make sure you're communicating important information to everyone it affects. This includes communicating your feelings to your family about not having enough help around the house, or telling your community that you want to have a community garden set up by the end of summer.	*Planning every second of free time* In business, most of us like to plan out exactly how the day will pan out. Down to the last fifteen minutes. Outside of work, we need to be more collaborative and flexible and embrace the terrifying lack of control.
Holistic thinking with a blend of empathy and compassion First off, if this isn't how you're running your business ... *have you learned nothing?!* Come see me. If this is how you're running your business, I think I've pressed this point enough. Blend your softer and more ambitious qualities to live in a holistic way. In short, allow yourself to be human.	*Not everything is a negotiation.* If you treat every decision as a win/ lose situation where you have to negotiate your terms, it's not going to go well. If you want to be happy, sometimes you will have to bite the proverbial bullet.

Settling Smart	Unconscious Settling
Thoughtfulness for the whole, not just the piece Always work with the whole in mind. In business, we are always mindful of how all the so-called cogs of the business fit together to run the well-oiled machine. Do the same outside of work. Be mindful of how one component impacts another. Don't isolate the various parts of your life in an attempt to bring order to chaos. You won't. All you're doing is ignoring the inevitable.	*Not everything is a calculated risk.* This builds off that last point, but to put it plainly, *don't treat every decision as you would a business decision*. You're going to have a bad time. Outside of work, have faith and take the leap. Hang the "calculated risk." That's just one giant leap of faith. Especially if you have kids.
Set better boundaries. Just because they're your family or your friends doesn't mean that they have exclusive rights to your time or space. Set clear boundaries that you need to maintain a happy, healthy person. If you know that you need thirty minutes when you get home from the office to just unwind, communicate that to your family. Be realistic about your needs and don't settle for what you think you should be doing or what people expect from you. You get to decide your boundaries—no one else.	*Logic + Rational – Intuition* *= Coming up short* Always operate on fact, not fiction/opinion. But once the facts have been set straight, don't ignore your intuition. Intuition is a very strong force that, when paired with reason and logic, will produce something unstoppable.

Design Versus Default

I'm quite certain that my philosophy on living your life by design not default and running your company the same way predates the whole design-thinking madness and adoption from technology, IDEO, and the Stanford D. School.

Design-thinking your life starts with empathy for yourself! This is where the quiz comes in, measuring your current state and helping you define your desired quality of life. Design and commit to the plan of action and test the iterative process of putting your plan into action. Don't be afraid if you need to shift forward or back along the way in order to continue to live the life you want fully and authentically across all five facets. We'll cover shift dynamics in more detail in the chapter of the same title.

Now, for another story.

While running another keynote, I featured amazing and brilliant leaders from the Fortune 500 to talk about the ways they recruit, retain, and utilize talent within their organizations. My key question to each panelist had to do with the mix of workforce/talent within their organizations. When I came to Microsoft, I asked them, "What is your percentage mix of workforce? Meaning, your talent pools made up of, full-time regular hires, and temp/contract/seasonal/intern/consulting workers?" They answered 45 percent [full-time hires] and 55 percent [all the rest; nonemployees]! Of course, I'd prepped the panelists that I'd ask this question so they'd come prepared with their percentages. Next, I threw a curve ball because I really wanted to know and so did the audience.

I asked, "Is that mix by design or default?"

The amazing and brilliant woman, without hesitation or reluctance, leaned into her mic and said, "Default." Well, no one else wanted me to ask them that question because—as is true with so many things within large complex corporations and our hectic personal lives outside of work—we more often than not operate by default instead of design. Think about it, we are reactive, and worse, we're caught off guard and even blindsided at times. When we actually use design-thinking principles, we're able to go for what it is we truly want, realistically and intentionally. By design, not default.

It's hard in my coaching practice or parenting of teens to say to them, "Okay, so you were surprised by that 'thing' that happened to you. What was your part in that?" I'm usually met with a deer-in-headlights look coupled with resentment. The truth is, if our eyes are wide open and we're navigating from the driver's seat of our own lives, it's rare that we're blindsided. Imagine that even though we know where the blind side on our cars is, for some reason we don't actively work around that by using mirrors, turning our heads, or even using our car's technology to alert us. You know the blind spot exists, so account for it by design. The risk may be so high, you will gladly keep it at the forefront of your decision-making and actions each and every time you get behind that wheel.

If you think about design-thinking process not only for your business but for the business of your life, it's beyond having a plan. It's knowing your options, iterating, blending art and science with creative and calculated risk-taking. It's studying endless examples of what works and what doesn't in front of your choice process, critical thinking, and actions.

Let me give you some examples.

1. A company has a recurring seasonal down period for the past ten years. They've become accustomed to it, it's predictive, and they plan for it. A design-thinking organization would get ahead of it and plan to pull it up through agile methods, creativity, and fact-based operations. They would break the seasonal slump.

2. If you have a victim mentality, you expect the worst, you "deserve" the worst, and no one in your family in the past five generations has ever had anything but the worst—and you perpetuate that into the future. Good for you. How's that working out for you?

3. A wildly successful entrepreneur takes on a big, hairy, audacious goal (shout out to Hallmark, Amazon.com, and Netflix). It's more than an idea or a feeling. It's rooted in the idea that "people want it, so let's give it to them." Designing

one's complete life is no different than designing a company, mission, service, or nonprofit. It all boils down to one simple principle: understanding what one really wants and giving it to that person (including yourself).

Takeaways Brought to You by Fact Versus Fiction:

Fiction #1: I can do it all if I put my mind to it.

Fact #1: It's completely and utterly unsustainable to Never Settle across all five facets. We are human, not machine. We're not meant to run this hard in multiple directions at one time.

Fiction #2: I can't do anything. No matter what, I always come up short in everything I try. I could always do more.

Fact #2: It's completely and utterly dangerous and devastating for you and all those around you who love and care about you to Always Settle across all five life facets. This is for victims. For most of us, thankfully, we have no idea what it truly is to be a victim. If you have been a victim or victimized, I am so sad to hear that and truly sorry. If we look at history, those who have come through horrific adversity have some way, somehow, risen above and dug deep into their inner strength reserves to make it out. Do not be a victim. There is absolutely no cheese down that maze. Moving your lever up one incremental notch at a time will result in a much more desirable life gem.

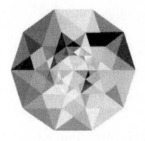

8

RELATIONSHIPS

RELATIONSHIPS, WHETHER FAMILIAL, friendly, or business, are vital. And it's because they are so important that we have to be careful who we choose to let into our world. It's time to do something that you have been told your whole life is wrong.

Be selfish.

Me before we. Oxygen mask on before helping others; there's a reason for this protocol.

The time we have is limited. So the people we spend our time with should be well worth our while. I know this sounds harsh but hear me out. To act completely out of self-interest is only a problem if it's detrimental or not in the best interest of another person. But this doesn't have to be the case. As oxymoronic as it sounds, you can be selfless and selfish at the same time. The key is to come from a place of honesty and kindness. Yes, you can be kind and selfish at the same time. Let me give you a couple examples.

The Business Scenario

You and a colleague have known each other for ages. You started out in the same company and, although you now work at different companies, you still grab lunch once a month and recommend each other's services to clients. But you're beginning to notice that your paths are diverging. The things that interest them that they like to focus on no longer benefit the people you send their way. And the work your clients are in need of bores your colleague. It's in your interest to change the dynamic of your relationship, both selfishly and selflessly. It's in your best interest to send your clients to someone who is passionate about the type of work your clients need. And it's in your colleague's best interest to take on work that they love.

Communicate your reasoning, of course, but stay true to what you know. By changing your relationship dynamic and investing less time in them, you selfishly do something beneficial for the both of you.

The Friendship Scenario

You meet a new acquaintance through a mutual friend. This new acquaintance is nice and a decent person. You like them, but you don't find you have much in common. Your conversations rarely evolve past chitchat. This acquaintance, however, really wants to become closer friends. They invite you out to lunch and drinks every week and find ways to strike up a conversation at gatherings.

You know you have no interest in furthering the relationship. Your time is valuable, and you prefer to spend it somewhere else. It's *not* in your or that person's best interest for you to force the friendship because you feel bad. If you force the relationship out of guilt, eventually it will turn into a toxic relationship where you're constantly burdened by a person's presence in your life whom you don't want there. And the other person, believing that you genuinely wanted to befriend them, will wind up hurt when you, inevitably, start making excuses and spending less and less time with them.

Save yourself the headache. Keep them in the Acquaintance Circle. Don't let them guilt their way up into your Inner Circle. Continue to be friendly but keep them where you are comfortable. For both your benefit.

The Family Scenario

Vacations are not vacations, they're trips! When you travel anywhere for the holidays, especially back home to where you originated from when you've moved elsewhere, it can get exhausting. For the first few years before my kids were born and after, we'd spread ourselves thin visiting everyone back home. We'd go from my in-laws to each of my parents, then possibly cousins, then over to my best friend's, then, to top it off, to see the people I used to babysit for who I mentioned back in Chapter 3. It was crazy.

After a few years of running ourselves ragged, we decided to stop the insane amount of family visits and progressive dinners, and just limit ourselves to visiting one family a year.

Take a moment to think about how you spend your holidays. Do you feel fulfilled at the end of your trip? Or do you feel as if you've wasted a week? Or merely met your obligations?

If you were to define your family vacation time, would you call it:

    a. Family hostage situation

    b. Definitely not a vacation

    c. Blissful

    d. Chaotic and hectic but totally worth it

e.   Other?

Avoidance is Not a Strategy

Oftentimes, relationships make us feel uncomfortable, especially if we have to deliver news to someone that they won't like. So what do we do? We avoid the situation, thinking (but really just wishing) that the problem will eventually solve itself.

This is rarely, if ever, the case.

Instead, the opposite tends to happen and the problem gets bigger and bigger until you're forced to confront it in an unpleasant way.

Avoiders and ostriches, it's time you faced the problem head on! Start by being conscious of the choices you're making. Come from a place of honesty and kindness but face the problem. It's your life. You have a choice.

Instead, don't avoid focusing on accountability, on your part and their part. Accountability is a universal differentiator. Hold yourself and others accountable in *all* relationships. Know that accountability done right is seldom a confrontation; it's a conversation with proof.

Just say no to multiple dinners and hometown visits crammed into a three-day period over a long weekend so that you don't have to disappoint anyone who expects to see you because you're "home."

The Power of Choice and Leadership

We underestimate how much power we have over our lives. Every decision and nondecision you make is a choice and it drives you. When we look at successful CEOs, it's easy to think they have it all figured out, that to them boundaries and relationships are inherent. This is not the case. At all.

To prove my point, I talked with Douglas Conant, the Founder of Conant Leadership and the former CEO of Campbell Soup Company, who led an incredible turnaround of that well-known brand by leveraging and working through relationships. I share our conversation in the hope that it will not only impart wisdom when it comes to having agency in your life, but will also illustrate that the power of choice will make you a better leader throughout your life.

On the topic of Settling until we realize that we have the power over where and when:

We have the power to choose between the stimulus and the response. You have the "responsibility" to make the choice. A response-ability, if you will, to the stimulus. It took me a long time to realize it in my own life. Before, I was running ragged on a treadmill while juggling my responsibilities. I was not anchored in what matters most. Instead, I prioritized everything equally. In the early days, with Steven Covey, I was working on my personal mission statement. As I was thinking about it I realized, <u>what matters most must never be at the mercy of what matters least.</u>[12]

Doug continued that until then, he'd thought his life balanced when in reality he was juggling too many things at once. That informed his journey moving forward. He identified the five most important things in his life: work, family, community, faith, and personal well-being. He gave up the pursuit of balance and traded it for the pursuit of fulfillment.

---

12 Conant, Douglas. Personal interview. 1 Jun. 2018.

On finding purpose in his work that continues his pursuit of fulfillment:

> For me, my purpose coming out of all my "work" is all about the people. The people I work with are part of world-class teams that are fulfilling and enduring! I discovered over the last twenty years at Nabisco and Campbell that great people are difficult to find. But we wanted the best. So, we identified, attracted, and retained the talent and leveraged them to their full potential so we could do extraordinary things, even beyond the four walls of the company. Our teams delivered world-class results. The most important factor we looked for in candidates was high competency, accountability, and chemistry. To put simply, people who would do what they say they'll do and who work well with the existing team.[13]

The choices that Douglas makes about the types of people he hires and leveraging them is how he makes the most out of his relationships at work. Selfishly. He wants to work with the best. So he seeks out and hires on people that have the potential to be great team members and leaders. In return, these people get to work in an environment that wants them to learn and grow as individuals, not just as employees.

On cultivating great leaders:

> When you lead a team from very high up you have to let the team function on its own. Somehow, people get trapped in tasks and minutia when 99 percent of decisions are happening when you're not in the room. And when it gets to you, it's

---

13 Conant, Douglas. Personal interview. 1 Jun. 2018.

completely re-imagined. You want that! Decisions on demand without you! You must build high-trust environments. To be a successful leader, you must meet or exceed expectation and be tough-minded on standards and tenderhearted on people. Truth is paramount as a leader. Even when things go wrong, as a leader, you must deliver results. Recognize what needs to be done and the timetable and plan for adequate time to deliver the expected results. In the beginning, it's a push. There's an art to doing this well. Handle the situation and your people with integrity and authenticity. Be clear on the standards you expect and have high standards. Mine tended to be even higher than those around and above me. My philosophy was, "Let's figure out how to beat our competitors at a minimum!" As a leader, you will make hard decisions. Tough decisions aren't necessarily popular but there are trade-offs. When we are clear and work through our teams, they will help us solve for this. They can help you make the best decisions in a difficult situation. Ideally, you want to be in a position where no one questions your intentions. You get here by building an emotional bank account with the organization. This will sustain you during tough times and hard decisions.[14]

Play to Your and Their Strengths

If any of you know me at all, you know I am a huge fan of Strengths Finder. If you've never heard of Strengths Finder, it's an assessment from CliftonStrengths and Tom Rath that helps you identify your top five strengths and focuses on playing to them rather

---

14 Conant, Douglas. Personal interview. 1 Jun. 2018.

than overcoming your weaknesses. Between my time in the corporate world and as a coach, I've probably used it more than nine hundred times. I use Strengths Finder as a baseline with all of my coaching clients. And what I've found is that it has no equal in showing people where they belong in terms of role, goal, and capabilities.

For Individuals

The reason I start with people's top five strengths, which I call their "secret weapon," is because it accelerates the process. It gives me real insight into what they bring to the table. And, while I have them take the assessment for corporate coaching, it extends to all aspects of their life as well.

Often, even though individuals are strong and at aligned companies, they're not growing in their career, they're stagnant, or they're just plain bored. Strengths Finder shows me where to harness and how to leverage their power. In some cases, along with additional data, it means moving them into a different role or function. Sometimes it means moving them up or out of a company.

For Teams and Companies

When it comes to a team dynamic, clashing personalities can cause a lot of misunderstandings and tension. I've created my own Strengths Finder decoder that helps me identify where people might have disagreeing working styles and what to do about it. But where there are opposites, there are complements. I'm able to see that and extrapolate correlating strengths. This makes teams more functional and productive.

When you have Strengths Finder and other complementary results from an entire group, team, or company, you can actually look down and across to see where you're missing strengths that might supplement what you're trying to do. For example, if you're light on Influencing strengths and traits, you might need them to evangelize your company or sell more of your product. If you're super-redundant, you probably lack creativity and are not necessarily set up for growth and innovation. There are so many varying combinations and permutations that can be tailored to each individual, team, or company. It accelerates my process significantly.

Embrace the Good

People are who they are and don't really change a lot without a ton of effort, coaching, and in some cases, therapy. People are who they are. They bring positive things to the table on their own. Employers need to harness this instead of spending time putting employees down, having them work on things that aren't working, and repeating constructive feedback in endless loops. It's demoralizing and damn-near useless. The problem is that often people don't know where their strengths lie. They know what they're passionate about.

Don't just tear people down. Help them out. Find their strengths and passion areas and put them in a position to excel by propping them up instead of tearing them down.

Takeaways Brought to You by Fact Versus Fiction:

Fiction #1: If I put myself first I'm selfish.

Fact #1: By being selfish, sometimes I create more energy and means to help and love others.

Fiction #2: Avoidance is a strategy.

Fact #2: Nope. Avoidance just delays the problem. It doesn't solve it.

Fiction #3: If you work on your weaknesses long and hard enough, they'll improve enough to become strengths.

Fact #3: Setting yourself and others up for success includes knowing your strengths and working with those, not working on your weaknesses.

Fiction #4: Performance Improvement Plans (PIPs) work.

Fact #4: Unfortunately, they don't. Because the one out of one hundred times a person makes it past their ninety-day PIP, they're so pissed off and demoralized, they either quit soon thereafter or end up back on another PIP later. If you haven't read *Radical Candor* by Kim Scott, check it out. She has some great methods for PIP alternatives. Basically, we need straight talk and to treat people we work with like grown-ups.

THE MOVEMENT

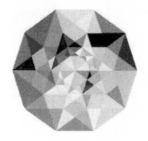

9

SHIFT DYNAMICS

THE MOVEMENT OF Stop Settling is one that is dynamic, flexible, and most importantly, achievable. It gets done because it's completely dependent on you and what you want. No ridiculous ideals. No unattainable goals. Just you, living your life how you want, situationally and relatively.

Change Is Dynamic

As you continue awake, aware, and Settling Smart, you're going to notice that the shifts that occur will not always be shifts forward. That is, the changes you'll go through in your quest to achieve your Desired Life Gem won't be linear. They'll move you forward, backward, and side to side. They may push you into first, second, or even third gear before taking it all and putting it in reverse.

This is natural. Don't be discouraged.

Stepping back is always the hardest part of changing: when the drive in you to move forward is so strong, but what you really need to do is step back, take inventory, and course-correct. Try and remember that this means you're taking the time to set yourself up for sustainable success.

I was coaching a young up-and-coming leader who had been on the fast track in her career and absolutely excelling in her coaching sessions. She took a promotion from an individual contributor to a people leader. She'd inherited some legacy challenges in both teams and processes, despite the incredible cleanup and subsequent growth plan she was able to implement during our coaching together. The revolving door of turnover she inherited would include some people she wanted to retain, and there would be blindsiding.

I'm a big believer in the "see it, say it" concept and have added my own stipulations to it: "see it, sense it, think it, feel it, say it."

So I warned her. I explained to her that I'd seen this before and eventually, someone or something would stop her and she'd fail. Granted, it was most likely going to be a Little F, but after succeeding and accelerating for so long, it would feel like a Big F. I told her it's natural and I wasn't trying to rain on her parade. I just didn't want her to be blindsided. When it eventually happened, she was upset but thankful I had warned her.

Instead of panicking, we deployed this three-step course-correction method.

1. Course correction
   - Weed out the problem, stop the Band-Aids, and fix what's really broken. Get to the bottom of the problem by channeling your inner two-year-old: ask "why" ad nauseam or at least until you reach the root of the problem. Way too often, we solve for the wrong things. We don't dig deep enough, and we stink at listening. We need to keep asking why something is broken or

not working until it gets a little uncomfortable. Then, ask again until you hit the root of what's really up with your client, friend, kid, fellow parishioner, etc.

- The best advice I was ever given in this regard was by a retired colonel who is like a father to me. He said, "Little angel, do you know why God gave you two eyes, two ears, and only one mouth?" In other words, keep your eyes and ears open and watch and listen twice as often as you speak.

- I'll never forget when I received a Women of Influence Award in Silicon Valley. All the women were asked to come up and receive their awards and share one bit of advice with the audience and fellow award winners. I shared that piece of advice and have been practicing it ever since.

2. Silver lining

- Finding silver linings are all about making room for progress to happen by understanding the lessons learned. There's always a silver lining in every cloud. Don't fool yourself into thinking that these bad things only happen to you. If you need to feel sorry for yourself, then time-box it. Give yourself thirty seconds. Set a stopwatch or timer and just feel sad, sorry, and/ or upset at your situation. Most of my clients never get past ten seconds. This is an awesome tool for your toolkit. It sure beats the alternative.

3. Get back on the horse
   - It's time to move forward. Once you know what needs to be resolved or improved and you understand that there's a good reason for it to be happening, get it done. Fix it, address it, resolve it, move through it then past it. And if at first you don't succeed, try, try again.

In that same vein, there's a toolkit to help you embrace and be equipped for the shift dynamics that will happen in your life. There are three main components to the Shift Dynamics Toolkit:

1. Slow Down to Speed Up (Or When You Feel the Need to Speed Up Slow Down)
2. Fact Versus Fiction/Opinion
3. The Platinum Rule

Slow Down to Speed Up

You will need to slow down. There's no two ways about it. As difficult as it is. As counterintuitive as it may seem. As excruciating as it is, especially in today's world of perpetual motion, you have to do it. Slowing down makes sure nothing falls through the cracks and you have a stable foundation to launch off of before accelerating to higher speeds. If you don't take the time and try to launch off of a wobbly foundation, you won't go far and it won't last long.

People like Patrick Lencioni and Kimi Werner, in their various works, have both championed the idea of slowing down to speed up.[15] And if you have not seen Kimi Werner's awe-inspiring story about swimming with sharks, go check it out.[16]

To illustrate my point about slowing down, let's get a little physical. And before you get ahead of yourself, I'm talking about physics. Woo!

Let's pretend you're driving a race car at extremely high speeds on a gravelly road. If you try and change directions without slowing down, while still going at a very high speed, you will not have enough interaction with the road to give you the force to change directions. The pebbles will spin out of your wheel. You will lose your foundation and spin out in the direction you were originally going. So, not only did you not turn, you just continued uncontrolled in the direction you were already going. And now you're sitting in the dirt on the side of the road wondering where it all went wrong.

This is also true in business. If you're already accelerating very quickly and decide to launch a new product or service, but don't take the time to slow down and make sure all the kinks are worked out and the teams promoting and working on the product/service fully understand it (read: have a solid foundation), you're going to eventually lose control or take a path you never intended to travel. There's no cheese down that maze.

Slowing down is a transitionary stage and is not meant to be a permanent state of being. You want to grow and move forward. That's the whole point! Staying competitive and ahead of the curve in a world that refuses to stand still long enough for you to do so. Plan to slow down, but also have a plan to get back up to speed once

15 Lencioni, Patrick. The Five Dysfunctions of a Team: A Leadership Fable. San Francisco, Jossey-Bass, 2002.

16 Werner, Kimi. "When you feel the need to speed up, slow down." YouTube, uploaded by TEDx Talks, 29 December 2014, https://www.youtube.com/watch?v=SFU_n1bSyyU.

you're ready. If the road is smooth, you still have to slow down but not as much and not for very long. The smoothness of the road (a stable foundation) will help you stay on course and keep your momentum going even if you decide to change directions. With a solid plan, team, and vision, you won't have to slow down as much when you want to execute a new project, sell a new service, or accelerate your growth; you'll have the foundation to take off much faster than your more wobbly competitors. Toeing the line between slowing down just enough to accelerate quickly and sustainably is a fine line that every business needs to walk to be successful.

Don't forget my personal account of going back to work after having a baby. Take the time to pull back, slow down, reassess, and focus on what matters most. Even if you need the income and/or love your work.

Don't Panic

Even with all the preparation in the world, you will encounter problems. They suck time and energy out of everyone when all you want is for it to *just work already*. They're especially aggravating when you're trying to accelerate by slowing down: whether they gunk up the gears and delay launches, products, and services; or you just found out the new house you bought has termites; or rabbits got into your community garden and ate everything. Don't let problems own you.

Own them.

Fact Versus Fiction/Opinion

Fact Versus Fiction/Opinion is one of the best ways to tackle problems head on. I use this approach with my coaching clients all the time to help them recognize where the real problems lie.

The formula works like this.

1. Before tackling any problem, stop and identify where the problem is originating. Is the problem based on cold hard facts, or opinions about those cold hard facts? Make a list of the different faces of the problem and label them as facts or fiction.

2. Dive deep into the fiction side of your list. What is causing the fiction? Why the emotional reaction? It's crucial to identify the why. That's how you get to the root cause. And don't stop when it gets uncomfortable. In fact, that's when it's most important to push forward. Keep asking why; keep pushing through until what you have is the root of the problem. The fact.

3. Now that you have your facts, work on solving them. Explore various options and anticipate their outcomes. Now that you're operating on facts, add in all the emotion you feel. As long as they come from a place of facts, they cannot be dismissed or ignored.

In practice, this can show up as a time when you didn't receive an expected promotion. It may be a fact that you have worked longer at the company than someone else, but it's probably fiction that your boss has it in for you. So you have your facts: no promotion and you've been there longer. Feel all you want as long as it's fact-based, otherwise you're wasting precious mental headspace.

How do you react?

You could use guilt to put pressure on your company: let your boss know how disappointed you are and that you felt you deserved the promotion for such and such reasons. But a more constructive route is more likely to get you what you want. Ask questions instead of playing the victim. What improvements or corrections do I need to make to prove that I'm ready for the next step? What is it that you're looking for in that position?

You have the right to be disappointed and angry, but make sure your emotions are stemming from a place of fact. Be absolutely positive that you're reacting to something real and not just a conjecture.

John Paller

I now want to introduce you to self-proclaimed "reformed douchebag"[17] and CEO of Opolis, John Paller. His choices and integrated life are a perfect example of being conscious and choosing how you live your life, spend your time, and make no apologies for the changes you make.

When talking about his pre-reformation days, it's like he's talking about a completely different person. He has stories of attending MTV's Spring Break in Lake Havasu with a specific goal in mind:

JP: The goal was to see how drunk I could get without getting arrested or dying. We spent a crazy amount of money on boats, bar tabs, etc. We spent more money on booze and parties in a week than we spent all year on books and school supplies. My acceptance and validation of myself was extrinsic.

---

17 Paller, John. Personal Interview. 26 Sept. 2018.

DLA: How did you end up founding your own staffing company?

JP: I started working in the recruiting space in '99. With my first commission check, I bought a lavish car and ordered twenty-two-inch chrome rims. I was the coolest guy in Colorado. I got exactly what I wanted from the car: popularity, chicks, VIP access. But none of it was fulfilling. In 2006, I started my own staffing company with the intentional goal of creating a better candidate experience. I was fed up with how most of these staffing companies treat humans like assets, cattle, inventory. You look at how the financial mechanics are set up, and there's a massive misalignment of incentive. Employers try to manage P&L [profit and loss] by cost of wages instead of worker productivity. So we started doing that. I incorporated my experiences and my moral beliefs into my business and it was the best outcome for everyone. My individual life started to become influenced by the way I was running my business world.

DLA: How did you achieve this transformation? What did you do once you realized you couldn't keep going the way you were?

JP: I had a mentor who cared about me as a person, not just a business transaction. It really caught my attention. Most of my experiences prior had been fully capitalistic business transactions and quid pro quo. But he genuinely cared about me as a person and loved me. It's weird to say that in a business context, but it was true. His actions toward me made me realize that I was being manipulative in my actions, friendships, and partnerships. They were all based on the principle of "I'll give you this. What are you going to give me in return?"

Once I began to realize this, it became abundantly clear that I had some business partners who I was not aligned with. I had to part ways with them.

DLA: So, now that you have shifted so far, what drives you?

JP: So, even with everything, I have no regrets. The way that I look at life and the reason I have no regrets is because every chapter of life is a predecessor to the next. And if you look back at the book of your life, you wouldn't have chapter thirty-two without chapter thirty-one or any of the other earlier chapters. They're all interdependent.

Democratization of employment really, intrinsically, motivates me. We really set out to create a better candidate experience. It became clear to me that there was massive friction between what was of value to employers and what was of value to the individual job seekers. And it's this determination and feeling that I was working toward something morally correct that has led me to be fulfilled and driven. When I make decisions, and I don't mean this as disrespect to anyone, I don't care what anybody thinks about my decisions in the context of my principles. Long term, every decision I make is not for short-term gain but for the advancement of the democratization of employment

I'm convinced that the future of employment is really not employer-centric but rather employee-centric. The freedom and flexibility of work is going to become the table stakes for companies. Now it's the quality of work and, frankly, purpose alignment. The new differentiation will be purpose and value alignment. There is no more productive person, relative to the individual, than when they're working on something that matters to them with respect to their values. If they're working toward something that is larger than them, that is more than a means-to-an-end paycheck, not that that's not important, we all need to make a living, than there's a clear and impactful purpose. The emergence of the purpose-economy is what I believe the next twenty-five years will be about.

DLA: If you're okay with it, I would like to play a quick word association game with you. Just to see how you respond to different parts of your life.

DLA: Money
JP: Tool
DLA: Should
JP: Values

DLA: Can't
JP: Break integrity

DLA: Work
JP: Purpose

DLA: Worker
JP: Entrepreneur[18]

---

18 Paller, John. Personal Interview. 26 Sept. 2018.

When it comes to the changes in your life, make no apologies for the choices and decisions you've made.

You're solving for the wrong thing. That is the norm, unfortunately. It happens in your marriage, it happens in your office, it happens at your church. You're solving for the wrong things because you're not clear on what the other person wants. You know why? Because they're not clear. Take the damn quiz.

Takeaways Brought to You by Fact Versus Fiction:

Fiction #1: Having quick answers is always best.

Fact #1: Even when you're right and even if you're right most of the time, smart enough to think ahead of others, and fast as a whip, pause! By really listening and playing back what you hear, sharing what you see, and checking in on others, you will get to the best possible outcome without casualties.

Fiction #2.1: Win/Lose is good enough.

Fiction #2.2: Lose/Lose, at least no one won.

Fact #2: Win/Win is the only win; everything else sucks.

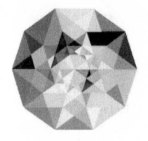

10

WHO ARE YOU?

THE QUESTION, "WHO are you?" sends a sickening shiver down most of our spines and causes a deeply suppressed existential crisis to crawl forward from the depths of our brains. But with all the millions of quotes, anecdotes, and self-help books that tell you how to set boundaries and live your life to your fullest, few of them ever mention how hard it is to answer two simple questions:

Who are you?

What it is that you want?

So, why is this so hard? I have a few theories.

Theory 1: Guilt

Guilt is felt by anyone who has a mother. It permeates our lives telling us how we should be living or what we should be valuing. Should. Should. Should. We're "shoulding" ourselves to death. I reject guilt as an emotion. It's manipulation and manufactured to make you think in a way that you may not otherwise. All the other emotions have equal options. Happy and Sad. Angry and Calm.

But the opposite of guilt is more guilt. You're not aiming to feel the antithesis of guilt. You're just trying not to feel guilt. It's ridiculous and yet so common. I mean just take a look at New Year's resolutions. If you're one of the few people that actually keep their New Year's resolution, I applaud you. But for the rest of us, it's just a way for us to feel guilty for setting out to do something that we felt we should do but didn't really want to do. If there's something you really want to do, you're not going to wait until New Year's to start.

Theory 2: Toxic Humility

There's a feeling that if we express what we want and who we really are, then we're boasting or bragging in some way. That by setting boundaries that others may disagree with, we're acting selfishly. As we've covered, that's not necessarily a bad thing. Act selfishly! Kindly and with honesty, but selfishly as well! Own who you are and make no apologies for what you cannot compromise. You're allowed to be you.

Theory 3: We don't put our oxygen mask on before helping others unless it's an emergency.

We've all sat through those lengthy plane-safety demonstrations where flight attendants act out how to use the various safety equipment on the plane to an audience who just wishes they could turn on their phones. These safety guidelines stress the importance of putting on your own oxygen mask before helping those around you. Why? Because you can't really help anyone if you're not taking care of yourself first. Helping others and creating bonds and communities is one of the most beautiful things we can do as human beings. But if we jump in to rescue everyone else while forgetting our life jacket, we'll drown before we get very far.

Theory 4: It's a moving target and therefore not worth tackling.

It's hard. Plain and simple. People change, it's inevitable. And to try and track yourself through all the changes life takes you through is not a simple task. Having to take inventory of how you're doing, making sure that your passions still lie in the same place as before, adjusting your life when you find that you've changed, are all really difficult tasks. It takes a lot of self-discipline and self-awareness to really understand who you are and what you want out of life. And who has time for that?

Theory 5: None of the above. Fill in your own damn blank.

These are just theories. If you have a better one, go with it!

It's astonishing the lengths to which we go to unnecessarily compromise who we are.

I have a colleague, and now client, who has a serious passion for art and museums. Whenever he's vacationing in a new city, he makes it a point to check out the local art museums. As luck would have it, a business trip took him to Paris for the first time. I was excited for him. The Louvre. The Musée d'Orsay. He would be able to see some of the most iconic museums and art of our time.

I called him while he was still in Paris and asked whether or not he'd visited the museums yet. He responded that since he was there to work, he didn't feel right visiting the museums. I asked him whether he was behind on work. No, he was all caught up.

133

"So, you're just sitting in your hotel room?"

"Yeah."

I wished I had a camera to look into like in an episode of "The Office."

I told him firmly that if he was all caught up on work and prepped for his meetings, then why on earth would he not take advantage of the opportunity to visit places he'd been yearning to see for years? Who would care? Who would have a problem with it? He'd get to indulge his passion and bring that excitement to the meetings the next day.

He finally relented and agreed to go out to the museums. And no one had an issue with it.

He was working sixteen-hour days. In fact, when he finally got up the courage to discuss this with his boss, his boss didn't care at all. He was only concerned with performance. The lesson learned is that the value you bring to your work, ideally showing up as the "whole" you and not some mask you wear, purporting to be a superhero. Heroism is a tall platform to fall off. And it's usually not by design. He was operating from a place of fiction, not fact.

Now, I'm not advocating that you try and use your company as your own personal travel agency. But if you are traveling, all caught up on your work, and prepped for whatever you need to do while there, why wouldn't you go out (on your own dime, of course) and do what makes you happy? We have this overwhelming feeling that we should be acting a certain way to meet someone else's expectations. The reality though is that, most of the time, those expectations are in our own heads. So when you ask yourself, "Am I living the life I really want?" The only right answer is the one that is true to you.

Core Values

Your core values are the ultimate way to define yourself. They are your non-negotiables and deal breakers. Your line in the sand. These values must be absolute and shift rarely if ever. Only after some deep self-reflection should you commit to any of them. They are the essence of who you are: mind, soul, and body.

My core values are integrity and making a difference. My deal breaker is negativity (others' and my own). And my tenacity makes me unique. If I believe in something I will never give up.

To find your core values, ask yourself the following questions:

1. What is my true north? What do I stand for?
2. What makes me unique?
3. What is my deal breaker?

When I was trying to nail down my core values, as someone who is very career- and achievement-driven, I was a little surprised to realize that power or money weren't part of my core values. I will never forget the day this came to a head for me when a brilliant founder I was working with became so frustrated with me because their motivation was money and wealth, and therefore power. But for me, in reality, all money is, is the freedom to choose. Just a tool that's a means to an end. I do believe that it makes you more or less of who you really are at your core. Or as the enigmatic John Paller, founder of Opolis, said, "Abundance of wealth is a by-product of value creation for other people."[19]

---

19 Paller, John. Personal Interview. 26 Sept. 2018.

You're Not Alone

Remember that bonus round question on the quiz? You know the one that I asked throughout my career and with all my friends and family to try and garner what's working and not for them and ultimately, what it is that you really and truly want? Here are the themes that have emerged from our quiz takers who were brave and authentic in answering this two-part question: If you had an endless bucket of money and a magic wand, what's the one thing you would start today?

Facet	Recurring Themes (Male and Female when known)
Career	M: Own business; entrepreneurship; advancing education; buying a house F: Own business; saving for the future; paying off bills; dream job; going to workshops; retiring; paying off school loans; remodeling; advancing education; spending less time on work
Generations and Circle	M: Spending more quality time with family & friends; being a better parent; planning better for kids' education; taking more family vacations F: Spending more time with family & friends; paying off debts; more social activities with friends
Society	M: Helping charities; increasing charitable giving; being more active in my community; creating programs that benefit the community and its members F: Working towards equality; volunteering; being more active with shelters; having more courage to stand up for others; focusing on being happy and giving; creating programs that benefit the community and its members
Vitality	M: Traveling; exercising; fishing; decrease stress F: Increase self-confidence; traveling; use time more efficiently and be more proactive; exercising; take more vacation time; pursue passions

If you had an endless bucket of money and a magic wand, what's the one thing you would stop today?

Facet	Recurring Themes (Male and Female when known)
Career	M: Working in an unsatisfying job; working for someone; working long hours; constant business trips; stressing about promotions F: Worrying about money/finances; stop impulse spending
Generations and Circle	M: Unfulfilling marriage; worrying about family's financial future; distancing family; stressing about keeping relationships F: Worrying about family; taking family on vacation; spoiling my kids; being in toxic relationships; not being true to self; people pleasing; fixing problems for family and friends
Society	M and F: Racism; sexism; hunger and poverty; child abuse; child illness; war; abuse to animals and humans
Vitality	M: Smoking; drinking; gambling; lying; ignoring my health; procrastinating on things I want to do and that are important to me F: Spending too much time cleaning; self-doubting; stressing; wasting time; being lazy; complaining; arguing; isolating; staying at home; putting others before myself

Who Are You?

Throughout the journey of writing this book, I talked with so many inspiring and incredible individuals. I feel blessed just having had the opportunity to get to know them even a little better.

I want to mention two amazing executive leaders who were kind enough to sit down with me, whose advice of pursuing their own happiness and fulfillment really embodies the Stop Settling movement.

Rosie O'Neill, Founder and CEO, Sugarfina

Rosie leads her life with a very simple mantra: do what you love and do it well. She's living proof that integration is possible. She serendipitously founded Sugarfina with her husband and they've worked together every day since.

DLA: How do you feel about work-life balance?

RO: By living your life as work and life, with a line down the middle, you inherently set yourself up for conflict. It's all about finding your life's work and integrating it in a healthy way! Love what you do and don't turn it off. It bothers me that, in my experience, the work-life balance question is always asked to women. Never to a man!

DLA: If you knew then what you know now, what is some advice you would give your younger self?

RO:

1. When you go after something, it needs to not feel like a real job.
4. Chase after your passion.
5. Sugarfina is a hobby that turned into a business. I would do it anyway if it wasn't successful as a business.[20]

Rosie is proof that if you dream it then you'll become it, as long as you're realistic and do the work. Growing up, she played with Barbie dolls and turned that into a career working as director of Barbie marketing for Mattel. Now, she's living the dream, running a successful company that embodies her passion for grown-up sweets.

---

20 O'Neill, Rosie. Personal Interview. 15 Mar. 2018.

Gary Campbell, President, Johnson Health Center and Founder and CEO of Impact2Lead

My next featured executive leader is my good friend, Gary Campbell. I test-drove the Stop Settling Method, Mindset, and Movement by speaking at his annual all-hands meeting for Johnson Health Center, as well as his Impact2Lead conference to help inspire people and reignite effective employee engagement and leadership development while minimizing burnout.

DLA: When you first joined Johnson Health Center, what was your intention in terms of the shift you brought to the team and patients?

GC: When I joined back in 2011, I spent three years as a director of HR and then COO. Within those three years, I saw how the culture was at the organization and how there were a lot of last-minute chaotic projects in the beginning. This was driving a lot of burnout and creating a fragmented culture. We started losing really good people. So when I took over as chief exec in 2014, the first mission was to become an employer and provider of choice. To do that, I decided to try to make it all about the employees. We had to break down a lot of barriers and unpack history, and really start to build a level of trust. Just to allow us to start to rebuild some credibility within the leadership ranks, community, and earn back our forces to take care of patients. We were named Employer of Choice in 2016, an incredibly distinguished and rare award, especially in healthcare, and it's still one of my proudest moments to this day.

DLA: Can you tell us why you started Impact2Lead? And how Johnson Health Center and Impact2Lead intertwine?

GC: They run in parallel and the Impact2Lead model is integrated into Johnson Health Center. The Impact2Lead model is built on providing value to others and putting others first. Leading with inspiration, making it personal, and creating trust. At the end of it, it's about being passionate about what you do. And this is where we got involved with Stop Settling. My passion was to always put the employee first. That was what really helped me drive success and helped Impact2Lead to become so successful. I now talk and train other companies, even some outside of the healthcare industry, all over the country on the Impact2Lead model and it was really possible because I followed my passion.

DLA: During an interview with *Modern Healthcare*, Doctor Kadree, reminded me to think about my own mission to help people build and realize their multifaceted selves. She said that I'd encouraged them to not be too risk-averse and to face the fear and to choose what works for them across their five facets.

GC: I don't recall exactly what she said but we are very much aligned about wanting people to reach their potential but not necessarily burn out while getting there. The Vitality piece is huge for her. She has four daughters spread all over the country. We're not a twenty-four-seven operation and it allows us to have other things in our lives. It helped her validate her thought process. From that she's taken a very active and passionate role in preventing provider burnout. She's extended this to the whole staff as well by looking at how to create better work processes. It really means something to her.

DLA: It's all about knowing where it is you want to make the tradeoff without feeling bad or guilty about it. It's great to go boldly into what works for you and allows you to have more space and energy to help others. It also struck me how you focus on humanness more than humanity. Would you elaborate on that?

GC: We are people first. We're mothers, sons, fathers, daughters, friends, family, we're that first. We care about each other in more than just a work context. We make it personal. We're all about being humane to one other and that we're caring and careful with one another.

You may be a kick-ass leader, a kick-ass mom/dad, a kick-ass person and still not lose your humanness. So long as you're coming from a place of authenticity, it's okay to have tough conversations; in fact they're vital. You just have to come from your heart.[21]

Both of these inspiring and amazing individuals are very Smart Settlers and they know who they are. Unapologetically. They have gone for what they want.

It's Not All About You

The challenge of discovering your core value and who you are is that it's actually incredibly simple but we complicate it so much that we need all this stuff to simply say no. The most successful people in the world are absolutely known for saying ten noes to every one yes.

---

21 Campbell, Gary. Personal Interview. 19 Oct. 2018.

How many noes do you say to every yes?

For me, this has been a struggle my entire life, especially in my career with employees. I've worked my way up to about five to one. And I'm pretty proud of that!

It's become clear to me over the years that when we think we're less, or push ourselves into being small, or into thinking and operating down, we're coming from a place of confidence issues. When we think others are more than us because of their title, the amount of money they have in their bank account, or the value of their house, we're coming from a place of less than.

It's wrong. We are all equal. We are all human beings. What we have has nothing to do with anything. It's who we are that counts.

As a fairly new corporate leader, I was asked to fire somebody within the first ninety days of my employment. I said no. I wanted to assess this person myself and make my own decision. I also wanted to see if I could figure out why he was failing and if I could find a different fit for him. I wasn't going to come in and just do somebody else's dirty work. It was curious to me that they hadn't done it themselves and left it to me as a new people leader.

Not only did I figure out why he was failing and what his strengths were, I was able to move him into a different role where he was able to really thrive. In the following year, he was named Employee of the Year for the entire corporate headquarters.

He went on to work for me at several different companies. Sadly, he ended up passing away at a very young age, leaving a young-adult child and two teenagers behind. It was such a terrible ending and so sudden. The family wasn't able to do the eulogy; it was too much for them, so I was able to honor him by doing the eulogy and helping out his family while getting some closure for myself. He was such a special person to me. In the end, he was like family.

What would've initially been an awful and unfair experience turned into an incredible friendship. Stop Settling by ensuring that you're giving everybody not only a fair chance, but also getting into their heads: figuring out what they're good at and what their strengths are, then helping set them up for success. Which in turn sets you up for success, which then sets your company up for success. It's a win-win-win.

When you're in a higher position and you have to let someone go for whatever reason, you're not greater than and they are not less than. Here's the trick: if you make it about them and not about you it will change the dynamic. It will allow you to be much more a giver and less a taker. Let me be clear: when you have to let someone go, for cause or otherwise, it sucks. I don't care if you're like me and you've done it one hundred times or you've done it once. It sucks. It even sucks when they've "earned the right" to be removed from the company because they've done something wrong, etc.

Here's the opportunity. Do not make it about you; make it about them.

Selfishness and selflessness are two sides of the same coin. Apply them appropriately.

Help them out the door with grace and dignity. Let them know what they did that didn't work and encourage them to find their highest good and best self on their journey. And if they're not being let go for cause, encourage them to find a place culturally and skill-wise that fits them the best. That's how you do something right for them as they're exiting your company and your working relationship. I cannot tell you how many times this has worked either for myself or for my coaching clients. And it slightly alleviates the stress for you of delivering bad news. Many people don't belong in the company or role they're in or in the position they've chosen. Even though it may be bad news short-term, it may be great news long-term.

Remember, it's not about you. I thank my good friend and colleague Teresa, who gave me that piece of advice and the b-slap I needed.

I was exiting the last company I ever worked for, or with, or ran. I was basically becoming a corporate defector. I was doing this as a three-month transition out of my president role and she was the incoming CEO. Thanks to her, it was the most harmonious breakup I ever had, and this is a great example of two women shoring each other up and taking care of each other. It was a beautiful thing and a framework to follow for any executive doing any succession planning. And yet, when it came time to have my going-away party, which I'd been looking forward to, I felt uneasy. I'd built this incredible team that I adored and they had become like an extended family to me. It was really bittersweet knowing I was going to leave the company and write this book. The knowledge that I wasn't going to return to the way of operating as I had been for all those years and I was departing from my team and partners was hard.

To Teresa's credit, at my karaoke-going-away party, which was exactly what I wanted, I kind of got cold feet. It was mostly my own emotions around the push and pull of the whole situation and also the fact that I was so in love with my team. It was really hard for me to think about departing. I also couldn't shake the impostor syndrome that had begun to creep up. Being in the limelight all night and having a party celebrating me felt overwhelming.

That's when Teresa said to me, "Dana, it's not about you."

I felt my whole world stop. My ego was really in the way. Not in a negative, egotistical kind of way but really the opposite. I somehow thought it would be too hard for me and too emotional for me. She was spot on. It was about them. It was a way to pay tribute to them and thank them. It wasn't about me. Imagine if I'd given in to my feelings and not shown up. Imagine if I'd canceled the party. Imagine if I'd not gotten over my own BS.

I would have missed out on an opportunity to honor them.

It ended up being one of the most fun and wonderful nights of my career. I still think about it: all the songs I sang and all the people coming out of their usual comfort zones to sing and dance. The warmth, the love, and the acknowledgment that was mutual was so beautiful.

Thank you, T. Thank you, Team. Thank you, all!

FINITO

THERE'S A HILARIOUS show on Netflix called *Girlfriends' Guide to Divorce*. In it one of the characters becomes fed up and expresses the frustration of the ruse of having it all by being your all: (she rants)

> I wish I had more confidence because I feel like I am failing. I have four kids at home and one of them is leaving soon ... I'm trying to steal time to work on my pitch between lice checks ... I mean, some of us feel like we can expand infinitely. That our energy is just limitless. But it is not! It has limits. And so you have to make choices. And then you disappoint people because *how can you not?* There are no shortcuts through this. Then there's all this guilt and shame about not being *everything* ... all those pieces of you are who you are. And you need to know who you are and accept it ... limits and all with no guilt or certainly no shame.[22]

---

22 "Rule No. 303: Burn That S... to the Ground." Girlfriends' Guide to Divorce. Bravo. 12 Jul. 2018. Television.

These final takeaways are real-life stories of beautifully articulated and exemplified Life Gems. Here are just two more to get you working on your own design and deployment strategy. And please, share yours as you progress; we are building a community of Smart Settlers! And no matter how your Current or Desired Life Gem looks today, whether it's currently primarily a Careerist, Family First, Social, Activist, or Green Machine, this is your one life.

Use Case #1:

In speaking to Paul, an HR executive leader friend of mine late in his career, not only did he "get it" in terms of Settling Smart, he actually showed me that there's Settling Smart within the facets and not just across them. He told me a story about how in college he remembered he went from killing himself to get all As to consciously trading off study time to enjoy campus life and get a couple of Bs. That way he'd have a little fun and a well-rounded collegiate experience. Today, as he winds down his very successful career, he has become a mastermind in designing his day to day, and here is what it looks like:

- Leaves house by 4:30 a.m.
- Drives forty-three miles in his commuter car
- Goes to Starbucks, has coffee and breakfast, and reads the Wall Street Journal in peace
- Gets into the office by 6:30 a.m.
- Leaves the office around 1:00 p.m.
- Treks back the forty-three miles
- Gets back online as needed with flexibility
- Outside of career, prioritizes riding bike and spending time with family and friends

Use Case #2:

My muse Kate, shared with me, an audience full of women in tech (and a few great men) that we simply don't have enough white space in our lives. By being one of the only women in tech back in the day at the chief executive level, and going onto to transform her life as her kids were growing up and out of the house and onto their own careers, she designed a life as a coach, consultant, and interim CEO/CFO/COO, wrote a book, found true love, and took up sailing. She figured out what was important to her, drew the line, and made it work!

Both of these stories have the ultimate trifecta: joy, productivity, and value.

Use Case #3 — Yours

Finally, I want to re-ask the ultimate question to get you started and keep you grounded on your Stop Settling journey. Think about everything you've learned throughout this book, what resonated and didn't.

If you had an endless bucket of money and a magic wand, what is one thing you would start and one thing you would stop, today?
START:

_____

_____

_____

_____

STOP:

_____

_____

_____

_____

Now, define each of the following in your words, not mine.

1. Career = _____

   _____

2. Generations = _____

   _____

3. Circle = _____

   _____

4. Society = _____

   _____

5. Vitality = _____

   _____

Now it's time to act on it! Use these as guidelines for what you want for your complete multifaceted life. Take the quiz and keep taking the quiz as you and your life situations and priorities change over time. Share your results with others whom you work with and for, and those closest to you. Get in alignment, Settle Smart, and get ready to live the life you really want. Then simply live it, your way!

ABOUT THE AUTHOR

DANA LOOK-ARIMOTO IS a leadership and executive coach, keynote speaker, the founder of Phoenix[5], and the inventor of Stop Settling®. A Silicon Valley Business Journal Woman of Influence and an SIA Global Power 150 for Women in Staffing, Dana has shifted from her twenty plus years of leading small to F500 corporations within the Talent Ecosystem. Today, she works with like-minded teams to up the ante toward the way we work and lead the voice of the new talent movement.